Bedtime Stories For Kids (2 in 1): Sleep Stories & Guided Meditation For Toddlers & Children To Help Fall Asleep, Overcome Anxiety & Insomnia + Relaxation & Mindfulness (Ages 2-6 3-5)

By Meditation Made Effortless

The Fantastic Elephant! Bedtime Stories for Kids: Fantasy Sleep Stories & Guided Meditation To Help Children & Toddlers Fall Asleep Fast, Develop Mindfulness& Relax (Ages 2-6 3-5)

By Meditation Made Effortless

Contents

Nobody Believes Winston (16min) 1

The Cutest Penguin (22min) 5

The Clumsy Prince (21min) 9

The Friendly Monster (16min) 13

The Dream Givers (19min) 17

Calm (16min) 21

Rhino Plays Soccer (16min) 23

Baby Bear Gets Lost (16min) 26

The Invisible Flower (17min) 30

Under The Sea (21min) 34

The Treasure Hunters (17min) 38

The Great Food Fight of 1884 (17min) 42

Anna Goes to the Moon (17min) 46

Lenora Saves the Forest (16min) 49

The Good Witch (20min) 52

The Robot Birthday Party (18min) 56

The Animals Say Goodnight (19min) 59

Nobody Believes Winston (16min)

When Winston went to bed, he thought about his day. It was hard being the boy that nobody believed. A lot of things had happened, but nobody believed him.

Just after breakfast, he had gone out to play in the yard. He was only out there for two minutes when four golden eagles swooped down and grabbed him. They whooshed him up into the air and flew around the town.

Winston was scared at first, but he soon found that he enjoyed flying, and he stuck his arms straight in front of him.

"Woohoo!" yelled Winston.

From high up in the sky, he could see the tops of all the houses. He could even see his own home. All of the people looked like ants from up amongst the clouds.

As he soared, he felt free. The sky was bluer than he ever remembered it, and the rivers and streams looked like long blue snakes.

When the eagles landed back in Winston's yard, he thanked them all. They bowed their feathered heads and flew away.

Winston went straight inside and told his mother what had happened.

"That's nice," said his mother.

It was obvious that she did not believe him.

Winston sighed. Adults often did not believe kids when it came to things like this. Perhaps, if they believed more, they might get to fly too.

Winston was hungry, so he was happy to find that his mother had prepared him a snack. He popped some blueberries into his mouth and crushed them with his teeth. He could feel the juice squirting around in his tongue.

When he went back outside, he saw the neighbor's dog walking along the fence like a tightrope walker.

Suddenly the neighbor's cat started bouncing up and down on the trampoline. It flipped three times in the air and flashed a broad smile at Winston.

There were squirrels in the tree, and they were swinging back and forth, flying between branches, and catching each other as they swung. It all looked just like a circus.

Winston quickly ran inside to get his father.
"Dad! Dad!" shouted Winston. "You have to come and see this."

It took a few minutes of convincing, but Winston's father eventually followed Winston outside to see what was happening.

When gets got outside, the dog was looking over the fence, his front paws perched on it. The cat was sleeping lazily on the trampoline. And, there were no squirrels anywhere.

"But, they were just here," said Winston.

"Sure they were," said his father.

Winston wished that his father had been quicker. Surely, he would have seen the animal circus if he had come outside quicker.

It was lunchtime, and Winston's mother had cut his sandwiches into triangles. They were his favorite, peanut butter and jelly.

Winston took big bites, and the peanut butter and jelly mixture smeared up his cheeks. He wiped it with the back of his hand, but that only smeared some onto his forehead.

After lunch, Winston took a walk into the forest at the back of his house. There as a small creek there that he loved to play in. He splashed and splooshed, taking his shoes off so that he could stomp around in the water.

Not long after arriving at the creek, a massive Viking longboat sailed down it. When they got to Winston, they invited him aboard. He did so willingly.

They sailed off to the ocean and looked for mysterious islands. Far from the land, the sea shone like precious gems, blues and greens and blacks, and spots of sparkling white.

The Vikings were ready to turn around when pirates attacked. A cannonball from a cannon narrowly missed them, and Winston helped the captain to turn the ship around and take them back to the creek.

Winston was happy to be safely back on dry land, and he waved to the Vikings as they went off on another adventure.

When Winston arrived at home, just in time for dinner, he thought about telling his parents what had happened, but they probably wouldn't believe him. Adults were not very good at believing things that didn't usually happen to them.

Dinner was cheesy pasta with lots of bright green broccoli. Winston pretended that the broccoli pieces were trees and that he was a giant.

After dinner, he went outside and saw that an actual giant was trying to eat the tree in his yard. "Don't do that," said Winston.

"Why not?" asked the giant.

"Because squirrels live there. You don't want to eat them, do you?" asked Winston with a smile.

"I guess not," said the giant. "Can I eat you instead?"

"Definitely not," said Winston.

"Why not?" asked the giant.

"Because I do not want to be eaten," said Winston.

"Yes, that makes sense," said the giant. "I would not want to be eaten either."

"Who are you talking to?" asked Winston's mother from the back door.

"A giant," said Winston. But, when he looked up, the giant had disappeared. He must have been scared of mothers.

"That's nice," said Winston's mother. "Come on in, it's time for bed."

Winston was tired after his eventful day, and he did not put up much of a fight. There would be time tomorrow for more fun, after all.

As he lay in bed, he thought about flying with eagles, watching an animal circus, sailing with Vikings, and talking with a giant. It had been a good day, though not as fun as when he had flown to the moon.

"Goodnight," said Winston's mother.

"Goodnight," said Winston.

"I love you," said Winston's mother.

"I love you too," said Winston.

His mother turned on his nightlight and closed the door. Winston lay in bed and thought about what tomorrow would hold.

Outside of his window, Winston could see the moon. Not everyone could see the moon's face, but Winston could.

The moon winked at Winston, and Winston winked back. After that, he fell into a deep sleep, full of dreams.

The Cutest Penguin (22min)

There is a legend amongst the penguins, and if you could speak penguin, you would know what it was.

Of course, people cannot speak the penguin language, so the legend is only known to them.

Pepe, the smallest penguin in her clan, knew the legend very well. Her grandmother had told her the story many times as she lay in bed at night.

She would read from her old book, crafted from the petals of the ice flowers, and written with squid ink.

The legend was that of the cutest penguin.

Somewhere out there, there was a penguin, and that penguin was the cutest penguin that was ever seen.

Pepe asked her grandmother who the cutest penguin was, but she did not know. The legend had been passed down from generation to generation, but no one had ever found the cutest penguin in the whole world.

So, Pepe decided to find the cutest penguin all by herself. When she woke up after a night full of sweet dreams, she went off in search of the mythical penguin, the cutest penguin in the world.

First, she checked her family. They were all very cute, but she did not think that they were the cutest in the world. Next, she checked all of her friends. She had to admit that she had some cute friends, but they were not the cutest in the world. Pepe knew that she had to widen her search.

She went to the ice cliffs next, where the tallest penguins would hang out. They liked to stand up as high as they could, and look out over the lands. From way up there, they could see to the farthest reaches of the world.

Pepe checked all of the penguins that were stood there, but she did not think that she had found the cutest one in the world, though they were all very tall.

"From all the way up here, have you ever seen the cutest penguin in the world?" asked Pepe.

"We have not," they answered.

Pepe was not put off, and she left to go and search for the cutest penguin in the world. The easiest way to get down from the ice cliffs was to slide down the giant ice slide on the other side of the cliffs.

Pepe slid down the massive slide with a cry of *woohoo!* She stuck her feet up in the air and laughed as the breeze whizzed past her face. It felt for a moment as if she were flying. When she got to the bottom, she tried to think where she wanted to go next. She decided to go to the fishing pools.

There were fishing pools close to where she and her family lived, and that was where they caught all of their fish. There were always lots of penguins at the fishing pools, and if she was going to find the cutest penguin in the world, there was a good chance that she would find it there.

Pepe waddled over the thick ice, seeing shadows down below. There were whales down there. They were large creatures, but they were friendly too. She had seen one once when she had been swimming, and it had swum with her for a while. It felt like swimming with a giant.

When Pepe reached the fishing pools, there were lots of penguins there. Some penguins were diving into the water, and some had little fishing rods, long strings attached to found pieces of wood.

There were lots of fish being caught, and Pepe looked forward to some delicious fish for dinner. Before that, though, she would find the cutest penguin in the world.

Pepe talked to a lot of the penguins that were there. None of them had seen the cutest penguin in the world. All of the penguins who were fishing were cute, but Pepe was sure that the cutest penguin in the world was not there.

Pepe's brother was there catching fish. She said a quick hello to him before she continued her quest. The sun was high in the sky, and Pepe enjoyed the warmth from the sky above and the coolness from the ice and snow below. Her next stop was the trading post.

On the far end of the west iceberg, there was a small dock. The penguin traders from the lands all around would come there and trade their goods. Sometimes they would trade fish, and other times they would trade beautiful trinkets, like colorful feathers and cool rocks. If anyone was going to know where the cutest penguin was, it would be them.

Perhaps, thought Pepe, the cutest penguin lives in a faraway land, and that is why I have never seen them.

Pepe got to the docks as a boat was pulling in. There were already three boats docked there, and one was just leaving. Pepe would often come down to the docks just to see the boats. Each one was a different shape and color.

She talked to some of the traders, asking them if they knew where the cutest penguin in the world lived. Each time, she received the same answer. Not one penguin knew where the cutest penguin in the world lived, and they had never met this penguin.

By the time she was done talking with the traders, the sun was starting to go down again. Soon, the light would disappear for the day, and she would have to go home. Perhaps, she would search again the next day.

There was only one person left to visit. The village elder.

The penguin elder was the oldest penguin in the village, and she had more knowledge than any other penguin. Pepe was hopeful that the penguin elder would know where the cutest penguin in the world was, but the elder had not left her home for years.

Maybe the cutest penguin in the world had visited the penguin elder, thought Pepe.

Pepe made the long journey to the center of the iceberg, where the penguin elder lived. In the middle of a vast snowy area, there was a small house. Pepe knocked on the door and was invited in.

"Hello," said Pepe. "I was hoping that you could help me to find the cutest penguin in the world."

"The cutest penguin in the world," said the elder. "Yes, I remember seeing her, but it has not been for a long time."

"So, she has come to see you?" asked Pepe excitedly.

"No, I always visited her," replied the elder.

"Where?" asked Pepe. She was becoming more and more excited that her journey could soon be over.

"In the middle of the frozen lake," said the elder.

"Really?" asked Pepe, barely able to contain herself. The froze lake was very close to the elder's house.

"I would go out there, and the cutest penguin was always there. I am sure that if you go out there, you will find her, Pepe," said the elder.

"Ok, thank you," said Pepe, running from the house.

As she ran towards the center of the frozen lake, she knew that there could be some disappointment. The elder had not visited the cutest penguin in the world for a long time, and the cutest penguin may have gone somewhere else.

When Pepe got to the center of the lake, she did find disappointment. There was no penguin there. No cute penguin. No ugly penguin. No penguin at all.

Pepe looked to the north and found nothing.

Pepe looked to the south to find no one.

Pepe looked to the east to find an empty scene.

Pepe looked to the west and did not see a soul.

Pepe even looked up, but only saw a bright blue sky streaked with the red and orange of the oncoming sunset.

Pepe was sad, she had not found the cutest penguin in the world. She hung her head in shame and looked down at her feet. It was then that she saw the most fantastic thing.

There, reflected in the ice, was the cutest penguin that she had ever seen. Pepe stared at the reflection in the ice and knew that she had found the cutest penguin in the world. Below her was the bravest penguin in the world, the most exciting penguin in the world, and the most resourceful penguin in the world.

Pepe smiled. She had finally found what she had been searching for. She also knew one other thing. When she brought her family, friends, and the rest of her penguin clan, they would all see the cutest penguin in the world.

Pepe went home with a smile.

The Clumsy Prince (21min)

There once lived a prince, and his name was Prince Julan. He was strong, brave, handsome, and very, very clumsy.

He was so clumsy that he once knocked over a cup of elderberry tea, and the tea spilled all over his sister's white dress.

There was also the time that he knocked over a statue, and the statue fell on the toe of the king.

Of course, everyone remembers the time that he sneezed so loudly that an old lady jumped up, did a somersault, and landed on a pig. The pig took off, and the old lady was never seen again. Though, there are some people who say that she lives deep in the forest, away from any potential sneezes.

Prince Julan had sat down for breakfast with his family when he knocked his fork from the table. It clattered to the floor with an awful noise. As he picked it up, his elbow hit his sister's cup of orange juice. The orange juice covered the table. Prince Julan jumped up to help, but he had somehow tucked the tablecloth into his pants, and it was yanked from the table. All of the plates, cups, glasses, and cutlery fell to the floor with an enormous crash.

The king shook his head and did not know what to do with his son. Prince Julan's heart was in the right place, but he could be extremely clumsy.

The door to the royal hall flew open, and a guard stepped in. He had a message for the king. The king took the message and read it. As he read the message, a plan formed in his mind.

"So," said the king with a large, booming voice. "Princess Lily has gone missing."

Princess Lily was the princess from the next kingdom, and Prince Julan really liked her.

"She was last seen taking a horse towards the mountains," continued the king. "She was on her way to visit her uncle, but she never reached him. Everyone is out searching for her, and they have asked for our help."

"I'll go, Father!" shouted Prince Julan. "I have spent hours in those mountains."

It was true, Prince Julan had spent hours in those mountains, but not by choice. Whenever he was riding between the two kingdoms, he always ended up becoming lost and would end up in the mountains.

"Okay," said the king. That had been his plan all along. He loved his son, but he was not sure if he could take more of his clumsiness. It would be nice to have time to fix everything in the castle.

"Oh, thank you, Father," said Prince Julan with excitement. He ran over to his father to shake his hand and accidentally stepped on his father's toes.

"Yow!" screamed the king.

When everyone had calmed down, a horse and supplies were found for Prince Julan. He had put on his suit of armor, though that had taken seven footmen, and four of them had become injured in the process.

When Prince Julan got onto his horse, he fell off immediately. He fell off three more times before someone managed to strap him to the horse. As they left the castle, the horse bumped into a pile of barrels, and the barrels crashed into the market, causing complete chaos.

Prince Julan quickened his pace, removing himself from whatever trouble was happening behind him.

"Okay," he said to himself. "I need to get into the mountains. Whenever I have tried to go to the mountains before, I have ended up in another kingdom and, whenever I have tried to get to another kingdom, I have always ended up in the mountains. So, I need to head as far away from the mountains as I can."

That is exactly what Prince Julan did. He tried his very best to stay as far from the mountains as possible and ended up completely lost in the mountains.

As he climbed the first mountain, he saw a small shack. He decided to rest there. The old woman who lived in the shack offered him a meal if he helped her to fetch water from the well. Prince Julan was happy to help.

After falling into the well three times, and causing a small flood, Prince Julan managed to bring back a bucketful of water, though he spilled most of that on the rug by the door. When he placed the bucket of water down on the table, there was barely a cupful left.

The old woman decided that she would get the water herself next time.

As they ate dinner together, the old woman told Prince Julan of the dragon that lived in the mountains. Prince Julan was sure that the dragon had stolen Princess Lily. He knew that he had to find the dragon. He also knew that he was scared, and he could not stop his knees from knocking together.

As he left the shack, he had a belly full of stew and fear. He did not want to throw up, so he calmed himself before getting back on his horse.

Prince Julan did not want to find a dragon. He was not sure that he would be able to fight a dragon. He was thinking about going home when he stumbled upon a cave. Above the cave was a large sign. The sign said:

The Dragon Lives Here!

Prince Julan felt the fear in his rise in his chest. He hoped that the dragon would not come outside. As he was thinking that, the dragon came outside.

"Aaaaaaaaaaaaaaaaaaaaah!" screamed Prince Julan.

"Hello," said the dragon. "I see that you have come to rescue the princess. Well, I have taken her so that she can clean my cave, and you are not getting her back."

Prince Julan was about to turn and run, but he knew that he had to be brave. He drew his sword from his belt and lifted it up. As he lifted it, the sword slipped from his grasp and clattered to the ground. The sword hit a rock, and the rock flew up into the air. By some miracle, the rock flew through the air and hit the dragon on the head.

"Ow!" screamed the dragon. "What did you do that for?"

"I…I…don't know," admitted Prince Julan. "Why did you steal the princess?"

"I don't know," said the dragon. "I need someone to clean my cave."

"Can't you clean it yourself?" asked Prince Julan.

"Well, yes, but it is very hard work," admitted the dragon.

"If you need some help, all you had to do was ask," said Prince Julan. "I'll help you clean your cave."

"You will?" asked the dragon.

"Yes, but only if you agree to release the princess. Stealing people is not the right thing to do," replied Prince Julan.

"Yes, you are probably right," said the dragon. "Okay, it's a deal. You help to clean my cave, and I'll release the princess."

Prince Julan set to work. He dusted, swept, tidied, cleaned, and organized. When he was done, he had managed to set fire to one of the walls, there was double the amount of dust, the dragon had lost all of his gold, and all of his furniture had mysteriously disappeared.

Prince Julan looked at what had done and sighed. He had tried to help, but it had all gone wrong.

"Please," started the dragon. "Please, take the princess and never return. I will clean my own cave from now on. I never realized that humans were such silly creatures. Please, please, please don't come back here."

"Okay," said Prince Julan. He took the princess by the hand, tripped on his way out, fell down the hill when he got outside, and fell off his horse four times before he was finally saddled. Princess Lily laughed.

When Prince Julan returned to his kingdom, after four days of being lost in the ocean, he was welcomed home as a hero.

Prince Julan went on many more adventures, though none as exciting as the dragon and the princess. He always tried to do the right thing, and even though he always caused some sort of accident, things usually worked themselves out.

The Friendly Monster (16min)

Rebecca had a monster under her bed.

The monster was friendly.

He was probably Rebecca's best friend in the whole wide world.

The monster's name was Oogle-Shoogle.

There was only one problem, Oogle-Shoogle always got Rebecca into trouble, especially at bedtime.

Rebecca had just gone to bed, and her parents had said goodnight when Oogle-Shoogle came out to play. You see, friendly monsters usually sleep through the day and stay awake all night. That can cause lots of problems.

Just as Rebecca was dozing off, Oogle-Shoogle came out to play.

Oogle-Shoogle was furry. Fur covered his body from head to toe, and his fur was bright purple. He had two twisty horns on his head, and they were both solid gold. He had a long green tongue, silver eyes, seven toes on each foot, and a long, swirly tail.

Oogle-Shoogle's favorite thing to do was give hugs, and he was very good at giving hugs.

"Good morning," said Oogle-Shoogle.

"It is night time," said Rebecca.

"Oh, yeah, I forgot," smiled Oogle-Shoogle. "So, do you want to play?"

" I can't play," reminded Rebecca. "It is time for me to go to sleep."

"Hmm," said Oogle-Shoogle. "I couldn't sleep today. I think that there was a monster in the closet."

" A monster in the closet?" asked Rebecca.

"Yes," stated Oogle-Shoogle. He licked his lips nervously. "I was in the closet earlier, and I think that I heard a monster in there."

"Wait," said Rebecca. "You were in the closet, and you thought that there was a monster in the closet?"

"Exactly," said Oogle-Shoogle. He folded his hands across his chest.

"Oogle-Shoogle," started Rebecca. "YOU were the monster in the closet."

"Oh, yeah!" shouted Oogle-Shoogle.

"Shh, my parents will hear us," said Rebecca.

"Let's jump on the bed," said Oogle-Shoogle with a big smile on his face.

Rebecca could not deny the monster his happiness, so she agreed to jump on the bed.

The two of them jumped up and down, boinging on the springs of the bed, whooping and hollering as loud as they could.

It was so much fun!

It was so much fun that Rebecca forgot about keeping quiet. It was supposed to be bedtime. Oogle-Shoogle should have known better, but he was much too good at getting into trouble to remember about bedtime for humans. He made even more noise.

When footsteps were heard on the stairs, Oogle-Shoogle quickly dived back under the bed, and Rebecca jumped under the covers. The room door opened, letting in light from the hallway. Rebecca tried to pretend that she was asleep, but he did not fool her parents.

"A lot of noise coming from up here," said her father.

"Sounded like someone was jumping on the bed," said her mother.

"Okay," started Rebecca, sitting up in bed. "It was not my fault. The monster under the bed made me do it."

"Oh, really," said her father. He bent down and looked under the bed. "Looks clear down there. Time to get some sleep, okay."

Rebecca pulled the blankets up around her neck and wriggled. When her parents had gone back downstairs, she slung herself over the side of the bed and peeked under. Oogle-Shoogle was not there.

"Oogle-Shoogle, are you in the closet?" asked Rebecca.

"Yes," whispered Oogle-Shoogle. He slowly opened the door. "Are they gone?"

"You can't get me into trouble like that," said Rebecca.

"Sorry," said Oogle-Shoogle. "It is just so much fun to play with you."

"It is fun to play with you, too," said Rebecca.

"Here, take this," said Oogle-Shoogle. He handed Rebecca a large tuba.

She tried to hold it up, but it fell to the ground with a tremendous clatter. Rebecca sat with her eyes wide open, listening for her parents. There was a thundering noise on the stairs. Right on cue, Oogle-Shoogle started blasting music with a trumpet, as if he were heralding the arrival of Rebecca's parents.

The room door flew open, bathing the room in light. Silence descended instantly. Rebecca was not sure exactly how it happened, but she was now holding the trumpet, with the end pressed to her lips. Her eyes darted around the room, looking for Oogle-Shoogle and the large tuba. Both were nowhere to be seen.

"As much as I love to hear you play your trumpet, Rebecca, do you think that this is the best time?" asked her mother.

"No," agreed Rebecca. She wanted to tell her mother about the monster and the tuba, but she could not find them anywhere, and Oogle-Shoogle was very good at hiding. It was better to just do what she was told and go to sleep.

Her parents went back downstairs, and Oogle-Shoogle crept out from behind the curtain. He was holding the giant tuba. Carefully, he stored the tuba under the bed.

"You know," said Rebecca. "When I need to sleep, a bedtime story always helps me to feel sleepy."

"Will you read me one?" asked Oogle-Shoogle.

"Even better, I will make one up, and tell it to you," smiled Rebecca.

"What is it about?" asked Oogle-Shoogle.

"It is about a monster who has a girl living under her bed," said Rebecca with satisfaction. She was proud to have thought of such an amusing story.

"It sounds scary," said Oogle-Shoogle.

"No, it is a friendly girl who lives under the bed.," said Rebecca.

"Like you?"

"Yes, like me."

Oogle-Shoogle sat on the edge of Rebecca's bed, and Rebecca started her story. By the time she was done, the friendly monster was fast asleep.

Rebecca cuddled up to Oogle-Shoogle and soon fell into a deep sleep full of dreams.

The Dream Givers (19min)

Have you ever wondered where dreams come from?

Many people have asked this, and it is commonly thought that dreams are created by our brains when we are asleep. Well, this may or may not be true. So, lay back, relax, and let me tell you the story of the dream givers.

Or, more specifically, one dream giver, Lenny, who was working his very first day in the dream delivery department.

When the story is done, you can make up your mind where dreams come from.

Lenny walked into the large building and marveled at what he saw. There were dreams of all shapes and sizes, all neatly arranged on large shelves that stretched as far as the eye could see. There were some who said that if you were to walk from one end of the dream warehouse to the other, it would take you a year.

Thankfully, Lenny did not have to walk all that way. He was only there to deliver the dreams, not to sort and categorize them.

Lenny was a dream giver. Dream givers are a lot like you and I. They have two legs, two arms, two eyes, two ears, but also two belly buttons. No one quite knows why they have two belly buttons.

Dream givers are also completely green. From head to toe, their skin is all green. And, not a pale green, or a sickly green, it is a light green like new grass in the springtime.

Lenny wanted to take one last look at the dream warehouse before he set off on his first nightly round. He walked among the shelves for a while, reaching out and touching a dream every so often.

This one flashed images of a circus in his mind. Trapeze artists were swinging from on high, a clown cycled around on a unicycle, and a woman rode a horse while firing an arrow at a target.

He touched another one and could smell a meadow on a summer day. There was the scent of lilacs, lavender, and lotus leaves. He could almost feel the warm glow of the sun on his skin.

The next dream was a little too scary for him, and he wondered why he had even touched it.

He quickly found a more pleasant dream, and he could feel himself flying across the sky. It was a wonderful feeling, and he did not want it to end, but a cough brought him from his dream.

"Hey," said Nora.

"Hey," said Lenny.

Nora had been delivering dreams for years, and she was very good at it. She had been tasked with taking Lenny out on his first dream delivery. She liked to help the new recruits. They were always eager to deliver dreams to the children.

Tonight, they were delivering dreams across Canada. They would visit some of the big cities, and then some smaller towns. They had all the addresses ready, and the dream workers in the warehouse were ready to give them the dreams.

"Are you ready?" asked Nora.

"Yes," squealed Lenny. "I am trying not to act too excited. Is it noticeable?" Lenny hopped up and down on the spot.

"You look the right amount of excited," said Nora. "In fact, you look exactly like I did on my first day of the job.

Nora handed Lenny his dream robe. Dream robes are colored with every color of the rainbow, and the colors shift and move as you wear them. Lenny took it and put it on with pride. Next, he was given his dream satchel. It looked like a regular brown satchel, but it could contain any dream in the world. He strapped it gently over his shoulder.

Finally, he was given his crystal communicator. It was a large crystal and could fit in the palm of your hand. If you talked into it, you could order dreams from the dream warehouse, and they would appear in the satchel.

"Shall we?" asked Nora with a small smile on her face.

"Yes, please," said Lenny.

The two of them set off through the magic portal and landed in Canada. They took off running. The night had just started, but they would have to be quick if they were to deliver all of the dreams on time.

At the first house, Nora took a look at the small boy sleeping in the bed and ordered a dream about riding on the back of an elephant. It appeared in the satchel, and she let it loose in the room. It would soon settle, and the boy would have a beautiful dream.

At the fifth house, Lenny was allowed to order a dream. He looked around the room. There was not much in there, and he was sure that the little girl lying peacefully asleep did not have a comfortable life.

"What do you reckon?" asked Nora.

"Looks like she has a tough life," said Lenny. "I think that I know just the thing." He lifted up the crystal and ordered a flying dream. As soon as he spoke the words, the dream appeared in his satchel.

Lenny reached in his hand, and, for a moment, he felt as if he was flying. He let the dream loose in the room, and left, happy that the girl would have a sweet dream before she woke up.

Nora and Lenny went from house to house, delivering dreams to all the boys and girls. They were almost halfway through the night when Nora picked up on something. They were in the room of a young girl. She must have only been six years old.

"Can you feel that?" asked Nora.

"I can," said Lenny. "It feels like she is going through a rough time and is having a hard time coping with it."

"What do you think we should do?" asked Nora.

"I think that we should find an extra-special dream," smiled Lenny.

"Hmm," thought Nora. "We could do that, but do you know that humans learn through dreams? A nice dream is an escape, but a tough dream builds strength and character. If we give this girl a tough dream, she may wake up a little scared, but she will build character and be able to deal with her real problems."

"I've never thought about it like that," said Lenny. "But, what if I give her a bad dream, and she finds out that it was me?"

"Don't worry," said Nora calmly. "Humans don't know about us. It's not like anyone is going to write a story about this. That is never going to happen."

"You're right," agreed Lenny. "No one is ever going to hear about this."

Lenny thought about it, and tried to find a dream that may be troubling, but would help the girl to overcome her problems. When he left the room, he felt sad that she would not have a dream about flying, or laughing, or playing. But, he hoped that she would find something helpful in the dream.

Nora and Lenny continued through the night. As the sun was rising, they planted the last dream. Nora drew up a portal, and they stepped through, back to the dream warehouse.

"So, how was your first night?" asked Nora.

"It was amazing," said Lenny. "I can't wait to do it again.

So, that is where dreams come from, or it could be. It's up to you to discover where your dreams come from. So, rest your head, close your eyes, and hope that Lenny brings you a dream about flying.

Calm (16min)

Sometimes it can be hard to get to sleep. You may have been playing all day, but you are still filled with energy. Maybe you ate some candy before bed, and it is fizzing around inside of you. Perhaps your muscles are sore from a long bike ride. Or, you might be thinking about something, and you cannot get it out of your mind.

No matter the reason for not being able to sleep, it can be annoying to lay awake for a long time.

One thing that you can do is to visualize a calming experience and immerse yourself in it. This means that you hold the thought in your mind and think about nothing else.

Let's try it.

Find a comfortable position and close your eyes. Try not to think about anything except for your breathing. Feel the way that your chest rises and falls as you breathe.

Now, wiggle your toes and fingers. Get all of that energy out. If you have a lot of energy, you can wriggle your entire body. Go ahead, do it now, wiggle your fingers and toes, or your whole body.

Keep going for five, four, three, two, one…and relax.

Keep your eyes closed and focus on your breathing again. Take slow breaths in and out, in and out.

Think about your legs, and rest them. Let the tension flow from every muscle until your legs are completely relaxed. Do the same for your arms. Give them a quick stretch, and then relax them. Let your shoulders relax too, and your neck and your head.

When you are fully relaxed, take three more breaths. In and out. In and out. In and out.

Now, we are ready to visualize.

Think about a meadow. There is green all around. There are green trees, green grass, and green flowers. Of course, the flowers are filled with lots of different colors too. You are in the middle of the meadow. Take the time to look around. You can see everything. There are some hills in the distance, and sheep and cows too. You can see clouds in the sky, and the bright, shining sun.

You can hear things too. There are birds in the trees, and they are chirping a beautiful song. There is a stream nearby, and you can hear the water babbling and gurgling. A breeze rustles through the trees, stirring the leaves. A cow moos in the distance.

Can you see the meadow in your mind? Can you imagine listening to all of those sounds?

What do you smell? The green grass smells fresh. A farmer has been by, and you can smell the cut grass too. There is a delicious smell in the air, lavender, and pine, and sweet honey. You take a moment to breathe in the air around you and take in all of the aromas. It is a beautiful day, and seeing, hearing, and smelling everything makes you happy.

What do you feel? The breeze that was rustling through the leaves is passing you by. You can feel the small hairs on your arms being tickled. It feels nice to have a cooling breeze, especially with the warm sun beating down. You decide to take your shoes off, and you can feel the fresh grass under your feet. You take a walk through the meadow to the stream and run your fingers through the water. The water feels cool and refreshing.

What can you taste? Did you bring anything to eat? Of course you did. You brought your favorite flavor of ice cream. Quick, you need to eat it before it melts and drips down your fingers. You lick the ice cream and feel the coolness of it in your mouth. The sweetness hits your tongue, and you can taste it. It is the best ice cream that you have ever had.

You decide to go for a walk. The hill in the distance is not so tall, and you get to view the surrounding area. A bee buzzes past your ear. A butterfly flaps its wings and dances around your head.

When you get to the small hill, there is a cow there, waiting for you. She lets you pat her head, and she is softer than you imagined. The cow trots off with a happy smile on her face. You continue walking until you get to the top of the hill.

From there, you can see out to the ocean. It is big and blue. It is also very calm, with small waves hitting the sandy shore. The waves flow onto the beach, wash across the sand, and flow back into the ocean. Try to match your breathing to the flow of the water. As the waves come in, take a breathe in. As they wash back out to the ocean, breathe out with a smile.

Now, it is time to come back from your mini-adventure. Take one more deep breath and, in your vision, close your eyes. Let your mind go blank while still feeling the warmth of the sun and the ice cream's sweetness.

It is time to take five more deep breaths. Stay relaxed and breathe in and out. In and out. In and out. In and out. And, one more time, in and out.

If you want, you can open your eyes and return to the real world, or you can keep your eyes closed and drift off to the land of dreams.

Now, when you are alone, you can do the same thing to calm yourself. You don't have to visit a meadow, though you can if you want to. Next time you visualize a mini adventure, let your mind take you wherever you want to go.

Goodnight.

Rhino Plays Soccer (16min)

Rocky was a rhino. And, just like most young rhinos, there was nothing that he liked to do more than to play soccer. If you were to ask him what his favorite thing to do was, he would bounce his soccer ball in front of him, and tell you how much he loved soccer.

He would go on to tell you all of his favorite soccer players, like Giannis, the giraffe, Leo, the lion, and Bella, the hippo. And, if you didn't stop him by changing the subject, he would talk for hours about soccer.

When Rocky was not talking about soccer, he was playing soccer. Sometimes he would play with his friends, and sometimes he would train alone.

This weekend was the final of the soccer tournament. Rocky and his team were in the final, and he was more excited than he had ever been.

He knew that he was going to have to play his best, so he was out in his yard practicing.

The first thing that he was practicing was his ball control skills. He put out some cones in a line, and he dribbled the ball in and out of the cones, using both feet.

After that, he found some goals and practiced hitting the crossbar. He placed the ball on the ground and tried to kick the ball against the horizontal bar at the top of the goal. This was a great technique for building his strength and accuracy.

Next, he found an even patch of grass and practiced juggling the ball, keeping it up in the air for as long as he could. He used his feet, knees, and head. His record was seven touches of the ball before it fell to the ground.

Before going back inside, he practiced his sprints. He had his father time his runs as he sprinted from one end of the field to the next.

When he was done, he was sure that he was ready for the tournament. He had practiced so much that he finally felt ready. Nothing could go wrong now.

The day of the tournament came, and Rocky was excited. He spent the entire ride there visualizing himself scoring the winning goal. He had done this before, and it had worked. He closed his eyes and saw himself heading the ball to score the winning goal.

When he arrived at the soccer field, the rest of his team was there. Susan, the pelican, played in goal. Walter, the beaver, and Sally, the giraffe, played defense. Arnold, the rabbit, and James, the tiger, played midfield. Finally, Rocky played in attack.

They warmed up a little bit, led by the coach. After jogging a few times around the field, the team came together for a team talk.

"This is it," said the coach. "You have the chance to do something special today, and I don't mean winning the tournament. Look at all of the people who are here to watch you. Your parents and friends are here. You owe it to them to try your hardest. So, what is our golden rule?"

"To have fun," they all shouted together.

Rocky knew that he was going to have fun, but he also wanted to win. He knew that they would, as he had practiced so much. He had put in so much effort, that he deserved to win. His coach had always told him to try his hardest, which is precisely what he did, both in training and in the games.

The referee blew the whistle to signal the start of the game, and the crowd went crazy. There were lots of animals there, some supporting Rocky's team, and some supporting the other team. Rocky wanted to make everyone proud.

The first half was a tight affair. Both teams had chances to score, but the two goalies were terrific and saved all of the shots. Then, not long before half time, the other team scored. Rocky could not believe it. He was trying his hardest, but his team was not winning.

Rocky tried even harder, but the other team scored again. It was 2-0.

Right before the halftime whistle, Rocky's team were awarded a corner. This was their chance. Arnold kicked the ball in from the corner flag, and Rocky, the rhino, rose majestically. As he soared towards the ball, he knew that he was going to score. He had practiced this move a thousand times. He had visualized it too. Absolutely nothing could go wrong.

Then it did go wrong.

Rocky missed the ball with his head and hit it, instead, with his sharp horn.

Pop!

The ball exploded.

The referee blew his whistle for halftime.

Rocky ran away. He had never been so embarrassed in his life. He hid down by the stream while the rest of his team searched for him.

It was his coach who finally found him. There were only a few minutes before the second half started, and they needed him.

"Well, that was something," said the coach.

"I'm so embarrassed," said Rocky. He folded his arms over his chest. "I've practiced so hard, and I failed. I can't believe that I did that."

"Yeah, it sucks," said the coach.
"Wait, aren't you going to comfort me and tell me that it wasn't my fault?" asked Rocky.

"But, it was your fault," said the coach.

Rocky could not believe that. He sat in silence for a moment before he spoke again. "I bet that they are all laughing at me."

"Yeah, they were laughing," smiled the coach.

That did not make Rocky feel any better.

"It was pretty funny," added the coach.

Rocky thought about it. He had to admit that it was pretty funny. The more that he thought about it, the more that he laughed. When the laughter stopped, the coach patted him on the shoulder. Rocky walked back to the soccer field.

When he got there, the crowd erupted into applause, and Rocky liked the attention, even if it was for popping the ball and not scoring a goal.

The second half started, and Rocky was happy again. Some of the crowd chanted his name when he got the ball. Rocky went on to score two goals. But that was not enough. Near the end of the game, the other team scored the winning goal, and the game finished 3-2.

Rocky was sad to have lost the game, but it would be a game that everyone remembered for a long time.

Next year, Rocky thought. Next year we will win the tournament.

Baby Bear Gets Lost (16min)

Baby Bear hopped and skipped as he held the hand of her mother. It was almost winter, and it would soon be time for them to hibernate. They would sleep all winter and wake up in spring when it was warm again.

Baby Bear was out with her parents. They were finding the last of the berries and eating them. They had eaten a lot of food over the past few weeks, and Baby Bear felt very full, though she knew that she would feel famished when she woke up after her long nap.

That is what her mother called the hibernation, the long nap. This was to be Baby Bear's first long nap, and she was excited to sleep for a long time.

"Mama, I'm going to go look for some berries over here," said Baby Bear.

"Okay, but stay close," said Mama Bear.

"Of course, Mama," said Baby Bear. She hopped and skipped some more as she went off in search of more berries. The dark blue berries were her favorite. They were not the sweetest berries, but there were the ones with the most taste to them.

Baby Bear splashed in a puddle, the mud streaking up her legs. She giggled as it dripped off of her fur. A butterfly fluttered by, and she ran off to chase it. She almost caught the large orange butterfly, but it swooped upwards at the last moment and got away.

When Baby Bear turned around, she could see that she was all alone. Her eyes closed together a little as she searched for her mama and daddy, and tears started to flow down her cheeks. Baby Bear was lost.

Then, it got even worse.

It was not supposed to snow for another two days, but large flakes started to drop from the sky. That made Baby Bear even more worried. She ran around on her little legs, trying to find her mother.

More snow fell, and everything was bathed in white. The snow blanketed the entire forest. The last of the leaves were covered, and the brown dirt was covered too. It was beautiful. But, Baby Bear could not see the beauty of it all. All she wanted was to get home for her long nap.

There was only one thing to do. She would have to make it home all by herself. Baby Bear wiped away the tears from her eyes and stood up a little taller. She knew the direction of her home and decided to start walking that way. She knew that she would either make it home, or her parents would find her.

What she didn't know was that she was going the wrong way.

After walking for a long time, Baby Bear got tired. She found some red berries on a tree. There were only three of them left, but it was better than nothing. After eating, she lay down on the ground and slept for a while. She had a small nap.

When Baby Bear woke up, she could feel that she was not alone.

"Mama!" Baby Bear shouted. She jumped up from her sleeping spot, but her mother was not there. Standing in front of her was a large wolf.

"Aaaaaaaaaaaaaaaaaah!" shouted Baby Bear.

"Eeeeeeeeeeeeeeeeek!" shouted the wolf.

Baby Bear took off running.

"Come back!" shouted the wolf, running after Baby Bear.

"No!" shouted Baby Bear. "You want to eat me."

"I don't want to eat you, I want to help you," said the wolf. He leaped in front of Baby Bear, and Baby Bear stopped in her tracks, afraid to move.

"Please don't eat me," whispered Baby Bear. She was shivering a little, even though she was not cold.

"I'm not going to eat you," said the wolf. "If I wanted to eat you, I would have done that while you were asleep, instead of watching over you."

This made Baby Bear feel a little better. "I am not far from home, I know it," said Baby Bear with confidence. "I only need to walk a little more, and I will get home."

"You do know that you are going the wrong way," said the wolf.

"Oh," said Baby Bear.

"Come on, we will get you home before night falls again," said the wolf.

The wolf took off, running in the opposite direction. Baby Bear followed.

They did not talk for a while. Baby Bear was feeling tired, but it was a different kind of tired feeling. It was a feeling that made her want to lay down, curl up, and sleep for a year.

"Thank you for helping me," said Baby Bear.

"I have children, too," said the wolf. "I don't know what I would do if I lost them. I am only doing what any parent would do."

They walked in silence again.

When the night began to fall, Baby Bear started to recognize her surroundings, and she knew that she was almost home. It was starting to get dark, and the moon was rising in the sky.

The wolf arched his back, raised his head to the sky, and howled at the moon.

"Awoooooooooooooo!"

"Why do you howl at the moon?" asked Baby Bear.

"I don't know," replied the wolf. "The moon is pretty cool."

When they heard footsteps, they both stopped. Baby Bear hid behind the wolf, and the wolf growled a protective growl. Two roars came from up ahead. Baby Bear recognized those roars. She jumped out from behind the wolf.

"Mama! Daddy!"

Baby Bear ran into her parent's arms.

"Oh, I am so glad to see you," said Mama Bear.

"We thought that you were lost forever," said Daddy Bear.

"I had some help getting home," admitted Baby Bear.

Mama bear looked over at the wolf. "Thank you for bringing our baby back to us."

The wolf smiled and ran off to find his family.

Baby Bear and her parents went back to their cave. They feasted on berries. When they were done eating, they all lay down together and cuddled to stay warm.

"Goodnight," said Mama Bear.

"Goodnight," said Daddy Bear.

"Goodnight," said Baby Bear.

Baby Bear yawned and stretched. She thought about her adventure with the wolf. She was glad to be home. Baby Bear's eyes closed, and she fell into a deep sleep. She would not wake up until spring arrived.

The Invisible Flower (17min)

Maggie was the smartest crow in the entire forest. She was a detective and had helped to solve many mysteries.

She had solved the mystery of the missing nest. It had fallen out of a tree and was hidden in a bush.

She had solved the mystery of the weird noises. It was the animals that were known as humans. They always made the most bizarre noises, but this time, they had been making crazy 'heeheehee 'sounds. No one knew why they did that.

She had also solved the mystery of the fallen tree. It had been a beaver that had chopped the tree down.

Now, she was about to solve her next mystery. The mystery of the invisible flower.

"So, tell me about this flower again," said Luke. Luke was Maggie's best friend. He was not as smart as Maggie, but he was very enthusiastic and would do everything that he could to help his friend.

"This map fluttered into my nest while I was sleeping," said Maggie, remembering being woken by the fluttering paper. "It marks the place where the invisible flower grows. If my calculations are correct, then it will bloom today. We have to go and find it."

"Let's go," said Luke.

The two crows took off from the branch with a 'caw 'and circled around the treetops. There was a slight warm breeze in the air, and it helped to lift them higher into the air. From up in the sky, they could see all of the trees in the forest. There were triangular-shaped dark green trees, large oak trees with bright green leaves, blue-green trees with needles instead of leaves, and silver birch trees with bright silver trunks and branches.

"Do you think that the invisible flower is one flower or lots of flowers that all look different, like the trees," asked Luke.

"I hope that there is more than one flower," replied Maggie as she soared through the air. "And I hope that they are all different, though we won't be able to see them."

Maggie glanced at the map in her beak and followed the directions. They swooped low over the poppy fields. Below them, there was an ocean of red.

"Do you think that the flowers will be rich in color, like the poppies?" asked Luke.

"I hope so," replied Maggie. She swooped lower to better see the red poppies. "I hope that the color is the richest color that we can imagine."

After the poppy fields, there were some farmer's fields. There were large patches of grass, and there were thousands of dandelions in the vast green squares, all bright yellow.

"Do you think that the invisible flower will have a color that is as bright as the yellow dandelions?" asked Luke.

"That only makes sense," replied Maggie. She could smell the dandelions below, and that smelled amazing. "This invisible flower is going to be the most beautiful thing in the world.

There was a lake at the end of the farmer's field, and it sparkled in the midday sun. The sun glinted on the little waves that were created by the slight breeze. It looked like a diamond on the of the water.

"Do you think that the flower will sparkle like the water?" asked Luke.

"Yes," replied Maggie, dipping her feet into the water as she flew over it. "I think that it will sparkle like the most precious gem."

The sweet smell of lavender wafted over the lake. Both of the crows breathed in deeply, enjoying the scent.

"Do you think that the flower will smell as sweet as this?" asked Luke.

"I think that it will smell even sweeter," replied Maggie. She was getting excited as they got closer to the spot on the map.

They flew through a wooded area, dodging in and out of the trees. Large mushrooms were growing out of the tree trunks.

"Do you think that the invisible flower will be easy to find, like the mushrooms growing on the tree bark, or do you think they will be like the small toadstools hidden in the underbrush." Luke had spotted the small red toadstools hidden where most would not be able to see them.

"I think that they will be hard to find," replied Maggie. "Things that are worth finding for are usually worth searching for."

Maggie flapped her wings and landed on a branch. Luke soon joined her. They took a moment to catch their breath, they had been flying for a long time.

"Are we close?" asked Luke.

"Yes, we are very close," said Maggie.

"I am very excited," tweeted Luke. "I have never seen an invisible flower before."

"I am not sure that you ever will," smiled Maggie.

Luke laughed. "Yes, that is true, but you know what I mean."

Maggie laughed too. "Yes, I do. Thank you for coming with me. I like having you on my adventures. You help a lot."

"I do?" Luke was confused. "But I haven't helped yet. I've only flown by your side."

"No, you have helped me a lot," said Maggie. "You have helped me imagine what this flower might look like, and that is a wonderful thing."

Luke was not quite sure what he meant, but he still puffed his chest out with pride. He knew that Maggie was smart and always spoke the truth. If she said that he had helped, then he knew that he had.

"Let's go and find this flower," said Luke.

"Follow me, it's not far."

Maggie took off, and Luke followed. After a few minutes, Maggie flapped her wings more slowly and landed on the soft ground. Luke landed too. They were in a clearing. The earth was bright brown, highlighted by the sun shining through the trees from above.

"They are here," said Maggie.

"There is more than one?" asked Luke.

"Yes, I am sure of it. I can sense them, and I am sure that they are beautiful." Maggie hopped forward, treading on the earth carefully. She moved cautiously as if she were stepping between flowers, but Luke could not see anything.

After a moment of searching, Maggie bent down and opened her beak. She plucked an invisible flower from the ground.

"I cannot see it," said Maggie, "but I imagine that it is the most beautiful flower in the world."

"It is the most glorious flower that I have *never* seen," smiled Luke.

"Then, you shall have it," said Maggie. She hopped over to Luke and passed the flower from her beak to his. Luke could feel the flower, and he beamed with more pride at being awarded it.

"Well," said Maggie. "Another mystery has been solved. "Let's go home."

The two crows flew home, and Luke had never felt happier.

Under The Sea (21min)

Melinda had lived her entire life under the sea. That would have been weird if she was a regular person, but she was a mermaid, so it was completely normal.

She lived with her family in a vast underwater cave with lots of rooms and tunnels. They lived so deep in the ocean that they could swim whenever they wanted and never be discovered by any deep-sea divers. Melinda would visit her friends, chase dolphins, and play kelp-ball.

Kelp-ball was a game that all young mer-people played. It is tough to explain how to play, especially if you have never played it. It is a game played with lots of seaweed, and it is a lot of fun if you are a mermaid or a merman.

Life at the bottom of the ocean was fun, and Melinda could not be happier. She did not want anything, nor did she need anything, but one thing did bother her, and it was because she was so curious.

She knew about the people who lived above the water, but she had never seen one of them. Her mother had told her that they did not have one tail like a mermaid did. Instead, they had two tails, and they balanced on them to get around. They were also not very good at swimming, and they needed special devices to come under the water.

"They would never come as deep as this," said her mother. "We are safe down here."

"I hope to see one someday," dreamed Melinda. She wrapped some seaweed around her hands and feet, ready to play kelp-ball.

"I hope that you don't, 'said her mother as if she were remembering something from her past. "They don't like that we get to live down here. I think that they are jealous of us."

Melinda didn't admit it, but she was a little jealous of them. She knew that she would never be able to live above the water, no matter what devices she had. That meant that she would never be able to discover all that the other side of the surface had to offer.

Melinda shook the thought from her mind. She tied a huge fish under each armpit and strapped a large lobster to her head. She was ready to play kelp-ball.

When she reached the large kelp fields, all of her friends were waiting for her. She could see that some of her friends had attached turtles to their backs, and she wished that she had thought of that, but she did have the lobster on her head, and no one else had that.

The kelp-ball game started. I would try and explain the rules to you so that you could better understand how it was played, but that would take at least three weeks. All that I will say is that the game involved a lot of bubbles, a volcanic eruption, and a shark attack. It was a pretty dull game of kelp-ball, as far as kelp-ball games went.

To make the game even more boring, the golden kelp was mishit and flew upwards. No one wanted to go and get it. Melinda's team was winning, and she didn't want to miss out on the chance of a victory, so she volunteered to go and get it.

"I'll be back before you know it," she sang, and off she went.

Melinda beat her large tail, propelling her through the water. She had a beautiful tale. It had the same blues and greens that were common in mermaid tails, but there were hints of pink here and there too. She loved her unique colors.

As she swam higher and higher, the water started to look lighter. She knew that the people on the other side of the surface had hung a giant light in the sky or something like that, and it brightened their world.

She hoped to see that one day too.

When she finally found the golden kelp, she had swum farther than she ever had. She thought about swimming until she got to the surface, but she knew better than that. She was about to turn around and go back down when she saw something out of the corner of her eye.

A surface dweller was there.

She swam away in fright, only looking back when she had reached a safe distance. She could see that it was not following her when she turned to look at the surface dweller. It looked like it was trapped. It was trying to free one of its tails from under a rock.

Melinda didn't know why she did it, but she swam back to help.

Well, you would get one of your tails stuck, wouldn't you? It's just silly to have two tails instead of one, thought Melinda.

When she got back to the surface sweller, she could see that it looked a lot like a merman, but with two weird tails instead of one beautiful one.

It looked at her with sad eyes, and she knew what was happening. The surface dweller had got its tail stuck, but, on top of that, its breathing device had almost stopped working. From the way he was motioning, she knew that it would not be quick enough to make it back to the surface.

"Well, how do you expect to swim fast with two bendy tails?" asked Melinda. She could see that it wore weird clothing on the end of its tails, probably to help it swim faster.

"I am going to help you," said Melinda. "Don't worry, I will get you to the surface."

The surface dweller seemed to understand, and it calmed down a little.

Melinda pulled the rocks away and freed the surface dweller. She held onto it and swam as fast as she could. She was proud of how fast she could swim, and she could see that the surface dweller was impressed too.
When they got to the surface, the surface dweller took off its mask and breathed in a large breath.

"Thank you," it said.

Melinda could kind of understand what it was saying, and she smiled. Then, she saw it. The massive light in the sky. It was so much bigger and brighter than she had ever imagined. She was so hypnotized by it, that she did not see the boat approach, not that she would have known what it was.

She only noticed it when it drew up alongside her. There were three more surface dwellers on the boat. They could not believe what they were seeing.

"We have to capture her!"

"We can put her in a museum!"

We can do tests on her!"

"We are going to be rich!"

Melinda turned around to see the other surface dwellers. One had grabbed a net, one had grabbed a hook, and one was waving its arms wildly in the air. Melinda could see from their faces that they meant her harm.

The surface dweller with the net was about to throw it when the one that she had saved knocked him from the boat.

Melinda knew that it was time to go.

"Thank you," she said to the surface dweller, and she was sure that it had understood what she had said.

Melinda dived back under the water and swam as fast as she could. She had seen many things. The bright light in the sky was amazing. She had also helped another being. She was not sure what would have happened to the surface dweller if it was not for her. And, without him, she was not sure what would have happened to her.

She made the decision to talk to her mother about it. She knew that her mother would be angry, but only because she would be worried. Her mother would understand, she knew it. She did not know what to make of the surface dwellers, they were confusing animals.

Yes, her mother would know what to do about it.

But, there were important things to worry about before that. She gripped the golden kelp in her hand and swam back to the kelp-ball field. She would not let the other team win.

When Melinda came back, the game resumed.
This time, the game was a lot more interesting, and I would explain it all to you, but you would probably be bored and fall asleep. All that I will say is that it involved nine blue whales, a thousand and one crabs, and three earthquakes.

The Treasure Hunters (17min)

"This is not going to be easy," said Lucy. She had a determined look on her face and was the kind of kid that could do anything when she put her mind to it.

Jodie and Carl stood in a huddle with Lucy. They were all five years old, and there was nothing that was impossible for them when they worked together. They had decided, three minutes ago, that they were going to be treasure hunters.

"So, we work together, and we find the yellow soccer ball," said Carl.

"The golden dragon egg," reminded Lucy. "That is the greatest treasure in the world."

"Right, right," said Carl. "The golden dragon egg."

"Let's do it!" shouted Jodie. That was all that she had ever said since she had started talking at two years old.

"We need to prepare ourselves," announced Lucy. She picked up a stick from the ground and handed it to Jodie. She picked up another stick and gave it to Carl. Finally, she picked up the third stick for herself.

The great thing about sticks is that they can be anything that you want them to be, and that is very handy when you are treasure hunting.

"I have a magical sword," chanted Lucy. She raised her sword into the air.

"I have a stick," announced Carl with a broad smile.

"Let's do this!" shouted Jodie.

Lucy led the way. She walked through the yard with her sword raised in case they ran into any trouble. Every so often, she would stop and wave her sword around as if she were fighting something. Carl did the same. Jodie put her stick in her mouth.

"Through the forest!" shouted Lucy.

"That's just a tree," claimed Carl.

"Use your imagination," said Lucy.

"Let's do this!" shouted Jodie.

Lucy led them through the forest, which really was just one tree. She made sure to check for bats and elves. There were not any, but that did not stop her from waving her sword around in the air. Carl waved his sword too, just in case. Jodie chewed some bark.

"Where to next?" asked Carl.

"We need to scale the cliffs of doom." Lucy made her voice deeper as she said this.

"You mean the garden fence?" asked Carl.

"No, the cliffs of doom," reminded Lucy.

"Oh, yeah, you kicked the ball over the fence," said Carl.

"Shh," replied Lucy.

"Let's do this!" should Jodie.

The three children approached the garden fence, which was also known as the cliffs of doom. The cliffs were not very tall, and all three of them had practiced scaling these cliffs. Jodie was the one with the least experience, so they helped her up first.

Lucy went next so that she could protect Jodie if she needed to. Jodie was chewing on her stick, and when Lucy got to the top of the cliffs, she helped Jodie hold her stick like a magical ice sword. That only made Lucy want to eat her sword more.

When Carl got to the top of the cliffs, the three of them balanced on top of the cliffs and surveyed the land beyond.

"I can't see it on the lawn," said Carl.

"That's not a lawn," said Lucy. "That is a wonderful meadow. We need to cross it, but watch out for the poisonous plants."

"You mean the dandelions?" asked Carl.

Lucy only shook her head.

"Let's do it!" shouted Jodie.

Lucy climbed down the other side of the cliffs first, before Jodie was helped down, and Carl followed. They stood at the bottom of the cliffs and looked out over the glorious meadow. It would take them a long time to cross.

"Do we have any supplies?" asked Lucy.

"I have a granola bar," said Carl.

"Good, let's have a bite each so that we have enough energy to make it all of the way across."

They sat for a moment at the bottom of the cliffs and ate together. When they were ready, they started walking. It would take them a long time to make it all of the way across the vast meadow. It did take them a long time. It took them exactly seven seconds. When they got to the other side, they were faced with three bushes.

"We need to search this forest of vines," announced Lucy.

"Let's do this!" shouted Jodie.

"Look, there is our yellow soccer ball!" shouted Carl.

"Golden dragon egg!" shouted Lucy.

Carl had found it. The dragon egg was hidden under a bush. Lucy ventured in and used her magic sword to pull the golden dragon egg from out of the hole in which it had rolled. She held the dragon egg aloft and basked in its glory.

Suddenly, there was a rumbling noise. A low growling noise coming from close to the large castle, which was, of course, just a regular house, but it was fun to pretend that it was a castle.

"The dog," whispered Carl.

"The dragon!" shouted Lucy.

"Let's do it!" shouted Jodie.

"We woke the dragon when we stole its golden egg," said Lucy. "We have to get out of here, or we will all be eaten by the dragon."

The three children ran back across the meadow. This time, it only took them three seconds to cross it.

Lucy was the first to scale the cliffs. Carl followed next.

"The dragon!" shouted Lucy.

The dragon bounded from the castle. It looked a lot like a large slobbering dog, but it was fun to pretend that it was a dragon.

"Quick!" shouted Lucy. She tried to grab Jodie, but Jodie was too far away.

The large, slobbery dog stopped in front of Jodie and licked her, covering her face in lots of dog slobber.

"Noooooooooooo!" shouted Lucy. "The dragon is eating her."

"Let's do this," Jodie whispered. The dog licked her again, and she giggled. The large dog licked her a third time and covered her entire face in slobber. Jodie only laughed more. She raised the stick in her hand and threw it. The dog chased after the stick.

Jodie climbed the fence and stood at the top with Lucy and Carl.

"You did it!" screamed Lucy. "The ice sword worked!"

The three children scaled back down the other side of the cliffs, made their way through the thick forest, and found themselves back at home.

"So, should we play some more soccer?" asked Carl.

"Okay," said Lucy.

The ball was placed on the grass, and the children started kicking it again. It only took three minutes for someone to kick the ball over the fence again.

"I guess we are going to have to go and get our ball again," said Carl.

"Follow me," announced Lucy. "We are treasure hunters in search of a golden dragon egg."

"Let's do it!" shouted Jodie.

The Great Food Fight of 1884 (17min)

The great food fight of 1884 is not often talked about. There are a lot of reasons for that, and it has come time for it to be recorded in history so that all children know what happened, and why the children of the past fought so hard.

There was once a time, long, long ago, when children were not allowed to play.

It was said that playing was a silly thing, and children should work instead, sit in the corner saying nothing, do chores, or something else equally boring.

For a long time, this is precisely what children did. They worked, did chores, sat in corners, and never played. That is until Bobby changed everything.

When no one was looking, he played. And, when he played, he found that it was a lot of fun. The more he played, the happier he became, and he came to realize that every child in the world should play.

But there was a problem. Adults only wanted children to do boring things. So, Bobby formed a plan. He gathered up all of the children he knew, armed them with all the food that he could find, and started a war.

So began the great food fight of 1884.

When it was found that the children wanted to play, the adults were not happy. They wanted children to only do boring things, so they formed their own army, and it was a very dull army.

The adults wore white clothes, while the children wore clothes of many colors. The adults stood in a straight line, while the children stood wherever they wanted. The adults did not carry any weapons because they were going to tell the children to go back to work. The children brought all of the food that they could find.

The adults did not smile. The children smiled a lot. The children even danced and sang and whooped and hollered. When the two armies were lined up on either side of the battlefield, the battle began.

"Stop!" ordered the adults. "Stop playing and go back to work!"

"No," said the children. They did not want to go back to work, they were having too much fun.

The flags were raised. The adults had completely black flags, while the children had rainbow flags, painted in every color. Once the flags were raised, the instruments were played.

The adults had one single drum. They beat it boringly. Beat. Beat. Beat.

The children pulled out trumpets and tooted them in silly songs. Toot! Tooty tooty toot! And the war started.

The adults stood there and gave stern looks because that is what adults did back then.

Bobby gave the word, and the archers were deployed.

The child archers were not like the archers that you may have seen in movies or on TV. They did not have bows. They had slingshots instead (some even used their hands). And, instead of having arrows, they had tomatoes.

The word was given, and the tomatoes were fired. The tomatoes flew through the air like streaks of red, some of the juice dripping down on the battlefield. The aim was straight and true, and the tomatoes hit the adults on the other side of the battlefield.

What were once white uniforms turned to splotches of red as the tomatoes hit and exploded. The adults grumbled about that. One even opened his mouth to shout, and a tomato landed in it.

Next, came the cakes. Bobby had helped to design large catapults. The cakes were loaded into the catapults, cupcakes into the smaller ones, and large birthday cakes into the larger ones. The children scooped up icing with their fingers and tasted it. The icing was sweet and delicious.

The cakes were fired. They flew through the air like only cakes can.

The adults saw them coming, and they did not move. The cakes splatted onto their heads with big splatting noises. Not only were they covered in redo tomatoes, but they were covered in cake icing too. Still, the adults did not move.

One adult stepped forward and said, "Stop this now. Stop smiling and having fun."

But, the children did not listen.

"Charge!" Bobby shouted.

The children picked up the rest of the food. There were cabbages, and hotdogs, and soup, and cheese, and peaches, and plums, and grapes, and eggs, and tofu, and chocolate, although most of the chocolate was eaten as the children ran with it.

When they got close, they threw the food at the adults. It was the last assault in the great food fight. The children threw all of the food at the adults until the adults were completely covered with food. From head to toe, the adults were covered in cheese, Brussels sprouts, sandwiches, corn, and more.

The children jumped up and down and celebrated. They had done it. Bobby raised his hand to calm everyone. He did not think that the battle was over. The adults were covered from head to toe in food, but they were still stood there.

Everyone stood and waited.

"You are in so much—"

"Hey, that was kind of fun," interrupted one of the adults.

"Yeah, it was kind of fun," said another. She licked some cheese and cupcakes from her face.

"No, no, it's not fun," said one adult, but no one listened to him.

Bobby was not sure what was happening, but he was convinced that it was a momentous occasion in the history of children across the world.

"But, look at them," pointed out one adult.

"Yeah, they are far too clean," agreed another.

"We should do something about that."

"Yeah, does anyone have any food?"

"I don't have food, but look over there!"

"Mud!" screamed the adults as one.

Bobby held up his hand. He was telling the children to stand firm. It was time for things to be reversed. He ordered the children to stand where they were while the adults grabbed handfuls of mud.

It did not take long for large mud pies to fly through the air and splat onto the heads of the children.

And, so started the great mud fight of 1884.

The children could only stand there for so long before they joined in. Soon, mud was flying between both armies, the children and the adults.

When the day was done, everyone was covered in mud, and everyone had a smile on their face. Well, everyone except for the one adult who still did not think that the food fight and mud fight was fun, but you can't please everyone.

And that is the story of the great food fight of 1884, which turned into the great mud fight of 1884. If it were not for Billy, children might still be doing boring stuff today. Because of him, children can play, and adults are fun too.

So, when you go to sleep tonight, think about Bobby and the great food fight.

Anna Goes to the Moon (17min)

Anna was a regular child. She liked to play, her favorite ice cream flavor was mint chocolate chip, and her favorite books were those with fairies in them.

She also loved the moon.

There was something about the moon that captivated her. Whenever the moon was in the sky, in the day or at night, she could not help but stare up at it and wonder what was up there. She knew that people had been there, but that had not been for a long time.

So, she decided that she would go up there and take a look.

When nighttime came, her father read her a bedtime story about a fairy who saved the forest and kissed her on the head. Anna went to sleep but reminded herself to wake up when the moon was highest in the sky.

When she woke, she could see the moon through her window. It almost looked like it had a face. She waved up at the moon, but the moon did not wave back.

Anna listened to make sure that her parents were in bed. They would not approve of a trip to the moon when it was so late, and she had school the next day. But, when else could you go to the moon? It usually came out at night, so that was the best time to go.

Anna crept out of bed and dressed for her trip to the moon. She did not know what she would be expected to wear, so she chose a sweater with a picture of the moon on it, her comfortable pants, and her extra-comfortable shoes. The moon was bumpy.

She had made herself a space helmet from an old plastic bowl, and she knew that there was a spaceship in her cupboard. She had found the spacecraft in her yard one day and had spent time fixing it up. It had a funny drawing on the controls.

"Now, where is it?" she mused a she looked through her closet. She reminded herself to clean out her closet so that she could find things easier. Anna finally found it at the back of the cupboard under some winter jackets. She was not sure if it would be cold on the moon, but she packed a coat, just in case.

Anna hauled the spaceship out of her window and onto the roof. She had not yet flown it, so she hoped that it worked. She was a smart girl, and she was confident that she had repaired it well.

Anna started a countdown. She did not need one, but she was nervous about going into space, and the countdown helped her calm herself.

"10…9…8…7…6…5…4…3…2…1…blastoff!"

Anna moved the control stick, and the spaceship lifted off from the rooftop. She could feel butterflies in her stomach as the spaceship lifted off and ascended up into the sky.

She could see her house and garden, and then she could see her neighborhood and then her whole town. The streetlights looked like fireflies. Soon, she could see her entire country, and there were patches of sparkling lights everywhere, like stars in the night sky. She looked up to check that the stars were still there. They were.

Not long after that, she could see the entire planet. She could not believe how small it looked from up there. It made her think about how tiny she was. The Earth seemed massive when she was on it, but now it was small in the vast universe. She shivered and wonderer if that would change her entire life.

"I am sure that it will. This is the type of thing that helps you to understand your place in the universe," said Anna.

She almost collided with the International Space Station. She had forgotten all about it. She knew that it was orbiting the Earth, but she had not expected to almost bump into it.

Anna moved the control stick to the side, and her spaceship swerved out of the way. On her way past, she could see the astronauts inside. They waved at her with stunned looks on their faces. They could not believe what they were seeing. Anna waved back.

From up in space, the stars looked brighter than they did when she was in her bedroom. She could see some of the planets too. Mars and Venus, and maybe Mercury.

The moon got closer and closer, and Anna was excited to get there. When she got close, she pressed the controls to slow her down. She landed on the moon with a tiny bump. She was glad to have her space helmet, it helped to protect her.

As she walked, she felt almost weightless. She bounced around on the planet, jumping in large bounds across the surface. It was a lot of fun. She also noticed that the moon was more yellow when she was on it.

"Hello."

Anna almost got the fright of her life. She turned around to see an alien. This was the first alien that she had ever seen.

"Hello," said Anna.

The alien had eight legs, like an octopus, but each leg looked like a human leg. It had no arms, a head with three eyes, and long purple hair.

"My name is Quiklert. I am seven," said the alien.

"My name is Anna, and I am seven too, it is a pleasure to meet you," said Anna.

The two of them danced around for a while.

"I am so glad that you came," said Quiklert. "I am the one who sent the spaceship for you. Did you get my message?"

Anna looked down at the piece of paper taped to the controls. She had not known that it was a message. She thought that it was a drawing, but it must have been a message in an alien language.

"I did get your message, but I did not understand it," admitted Anna.

"That is okay," said Quiklert. "As you can see, the moon is made completely of cheese. That is what we eat. There is only one problem. We are out of crackers. That is why I sent the spaceship. When humans visited many years ago, they left some crackers, but we have run out."

"Oh," said Anna. "Yes, that is a problem."

"What should we do?" asked Quiklert.

"I will have to come back," said Anna. "I will go home and sleep and, when tomorrow comes, I will find some crackers and deliver them to you when night falls."

"Yay!" shouted Quicklert.

The two children played for a while. Anna took some moon cheese home with her and planned to bring some crackers back the next night. From that moment on, she became the official cracker supplier of the moon.

Her parents did not believe her at first, but when they tasted the moon cheese, they knew that she was telling the truth.

Anna continued to deliver crackers to the moon until she was a hundred and one.

Lenora Saves the Forest (16min)

Lenora was a fairy. She was as small as a mouse and had large wings on her back. She had two sets of wings, and they were each a different color. One set was red, and the other was blue. When the light shone on them, they became translucent, and the light flowed through the thin wing material, emerging with a tint that reflected in puddles on bright days.

Lenora did not have a care in the world.

"I do not have a care in the world," said Lenora to her friends.

"We do not have a care in the world, either," they sang. "Everything is beautiful, and everything is pleasant."

And, that was true. They lived in a vast forest, and everything was beautiful, and everything was pleasant.

They would fill their days by flying around, hiding under toadstools, and planting invisible flowers. These were the best days of their lives. Until everything changed.

Lenora had seen humans before, but fairies had always kept away from them, and humans had always stayed away from the fairy worlds. Until they came hacking in with their tools and their noise.

Lenora was woken from her fairy sleep by the noises. It sounded like a waterfall, only a hundred times louder, and a squeaking mouse, only a thousand times more squeaky. When she went to check it out, she could see that they were cutting down the trees.

Lenora quickly found her friends.

"They are cutting down the trees," she said.

"Why would they do that?" asked Motgan.

"I have no idea," said Lenora. "Don't they know that the trees are our homes."

"What should we do?" asked Featherdown.

"We need to fight back," said Lenora.

The Fairies assembled in as large a number as they could. They found as many weapons as they could find, dandelion stalks, small pebbles, tree bark, and juniper berries. When they were ready, Lenora led the charge.

They could not let the humans cut down all of the trees, or they would have nowhere to live.

When they got close to the humans, they could hear the terrible noises. They could also see the trees shaking. The fairies had to dodge out of the way as a tree fell straight for them. When they were close enough, Lenora shouted, "Charge!"

They flew at the humans, waving their dandelion stalks and tree bark, and throwing the pebbles and juniper berries. It did not seem to trouble the humans at all, and they waved their tools around and swatted at the fairies.

"Retreat!" shouted Lenora.

The fairies flew away, finding safety in the trees that were not being chopped down.

"We can't stop them," said Bob.

All of the fairies flew away, except for Lenora. She sat and thought. When Featherdown came to visit later, she brought some dewdrops and treebeard. They sat and ate together.

"The fairies are leaving," said Featherdown.

"What!" Lenora was surprised, but she understood.

"They are going to lose their homes, so they are moving to another forest," said Featherdown.

" But, we have lived here for generations," said Lenora.

Featherdown nodded her head, and the two fairies sat in silence for a while. Once they were done eating, Featherdown flew away to pack her stuff. Lenora wanted to wait before doing the same. She watched her friend fly away and sat on the branch. She thought long and hard.

Why are they cutting down the trees? The thought ran around in her mind.

She wanted to watch them some more, so she used her fairy magic to stay concealed, and landed as close to the humans as possible.

Not only did their tools make weird noises, but the humans did too. When they opened their mouths, they made deep, booming noises that she could not understand. Still, they continued to cut down trees.

Lenora continued to watch them, and she discovered a funny thing. Whenever someone joined the group, they would raise their hand and make a noise. They always made the same noise. When they left the group, they would raise their hand and make another noise, which was always the same.

Lenora, the fairy, wondered if they were communicating. The fairies had always known that the humans were a silly race, but they did not think that they could talk to each other. They always assumed that the humans made silly noises for fun.

The more that Lenora watched, the more that she came to understand the humans. She learned that they had specific words for each other and for their tools. She watched them long into the night and into the next day too.

"Are you ready to leave?" asked Featherdown. The entire fairy clan was ready to go.

"Not yet," said Lenora. "I think that I can talk to them."

"What? But everyone knows that humans can't talk," said Featherdown. "Wait! Where are you going! You are going to get hurt."

Lenore flew from her branch and flapped her wings so that she was hovering in the middle of the humans. One human raised his hand to swat her away, but she spoke before he could.

"Hello," said Lenora.

Lenora was not sure if the humans were more stunned to hear a fairy talk or if she was more shocked that they could understand her. The humans lowered their tools and looked at the fairy with curiosity.

It took a long time to talk as Lenora had not mastered all of the human words. Featherdown watched from her branch, not understanding anything that was being said. Eventually, Lenora returned to Featherdown.

"They want to cut down our houses so that they can make their own houses," said Lenora.

"What are we going to do?" asked Featherdown.

"I am going to lead them to the forest where no one lives," said Lenora. "Then, they can take what they need without upsetting other living creatures."

That was the day that the fairies started helping the humans, and it was also the day that Lenora saved the forest.

After that, she decided to learn all of the languages of the world. She had discovered that there were many different languages that the humans spoke, and there were also lots of animal languages and nature languages.

If Lenora could save her forest with a few words, she was sure that she could do something special with a lot of words.

The Good Witch (20min)

Agnes was a witch.

She wasn't one of those old witches that you often read about in stories. She did not have wrinkly skin or a long pointed nose, though she did have a wart on her nose. She also wore long black robes and a pointy black hat, so she was a little like the witches that you read about in stories.

She did not have a black cat. No, she had a white cat.

Agnes was also a good witch. Yes, there are good witches. In fact, there are many of them all around the world, doing good things to help people. They often do this in secret. The next time that something good happens to you have a look around you for a good witch.

Agnes was working on something big. She was on the verge of a discovery that could change the world. She only needed to find the right ingredients for her cauldron.

Yes, Agnes had a cauldron that she would mix potions in. She also had a broomstick that she would fly on. Occasionally, Agnes would turn people into frogs, but only if they were really, really naughty.

"Hmm," said Agnes as she tasted the contents of her cauldron. "There are a few ingredients that are missing." She wrote the ingredients down on a piece of paper, grabbed her broom, and flew out of her small wooden shack in the forest. I have to admit that she was a pretty stereotypical witch, as far as witches go.

"Wheeeeeeeeee!" Agnes screamed as she flew through the sky. She always loved flying on her broom.

Her first stop was Mount Everest.

There is a flower that blooms on top of Mount Everest, but it only blooms once a year, and only when the moon is full. Not many people have seen the Everest Moon flower.

Agnes braved the cold, flying higher and higher, the air getting thinner and thinner. The mountain was covered in snow, and some eagles were circling near to the top. Agnes said hello to the birds (she knows all the bird languages) and swooped down to land in the snow.

As the moon rose a little higher, the Everest Moon flower bloomed, and Agnes took a petal. She placed it in her bag and looked at the next item on her list.

"Lava from a volcano that is about to erupt," said Agnes.

She knew just the spot. There was a volcano in the middle of the ocean that was due to erupt in thirty minutes. She took a look at her watch, witches still need watches, and jumped back onto her broom.

The eagles flew with her for a while, enjoying the moon's glow and the sparkling of the stars. When they left to hunt for food, Agnes pushed on faster. She knew it would not be long before the volcano would explode, and she did not want to be inside it when it did.

"These are new robes," muttered Agnes.

When the volcano came into view, there was a large plume of smoke rising from its center. There was also an ominous red glow coming from inside. She would have to be quick.

Grabbing her lava scooper from inside her bag, she flew as fast as her broom would take her, flying inside of the volcano, and down towards the molten lava. She scooped the lava with one hand, hanging upside-down on her broomstick with the other.

As she lifted off from the volcano, it erupted, red-hot lava spewing from the top. It almost caught Agnes's robes, but she made it out just in time.

"What is next?" asked Agnes.

She looked at her list. She needed to pluck a strand of wool from a new-born lamb that had been named *lamby*. She checked her book of predictions. There was a lamb that was about to be born in New Zealand, and the farmer would name the lamb, *lamby*.

She could take her time with this one, and she enjoyed flying over the vast ocean, the giant waves rising up and down below her. It reminded her that she had a swimming lesson in the morning. She did love to swim. Not a lot of people know this, but witches are excellent swimmers.

When she reached New Zealand, she headed straight for the barn. As she was perched on top, she watched the farmer emerge with a smile on his face. When he was gone, she crept inside and found the baby lamb.

Using her wand, she extracted a strand of wool.

"Magic magic is so cool. Magic, magic, come here wool."

The wool lifted from the lamb as it slept. She put the wool in her bag and checked her list. There was only one more ingredient to get.

"Chocolate chips," said Agnes.

This was the hardest ingredient to find as she would have to find a store that was open, go into it, and buy the chocolate chips. It was much harder than getting lava from a volcano.

Agnes, the witch, lived in Scotland, so she decided to head back to her home country and find a store there. When she arrived back in Scotland, she found a store and landed close to it. She hid her broomstick, found her money purse, and bought some chocolate chips.

It was one of the hardest things that she had ever done in her life.
Back in her wooden shack, she added the ingredients to the cauldron.

"Cold, cold, cold, cold. Bring about a flavor bold."

Agnes added the Everest Moon flower to the bubbling mixture. She watched with fascination as snowflakes flew up from the cauldron before falling back down again. She gave a smile and mixed the liquid inside.

Fire, fire, fire, fire. Your taste is something I desire."

Agnes added the lava to the cauldron. The mixture inside bubbled and swirled. Agnes took a step back as the mixture exploded, flying upwards like a volcano, bright orange and red, before it crashed back down into the cauldron and turned a purple color.

Agnes smiled. It was all working exactly as it should.

"New lamb, new lamb. Make the mixture calm, calm, calm."

Ages held the strand of wool between her finger and thumb before she dropped it into the cauldron. The mixture stopped bubbling. The surface became calm and reflected Agnes's face. She smiled down at herself and watched as the entire surface bubbled up in one massive bubble, growing to twice the cauldron's size before popping. The mixture calmed again.

"Chocolate chips, chocolate chips. I like chocolate chips."

This was the most dangerous ingredient of all. Agnes carefully sprinkled some chocolate chips into her palm. She looked down into the mixture, took a deep breath, turned her hand, and opened her fingers. The chocolate chips fell down like tiny black rocks, each splashing with small splashes.

Agnes jumped back and shielded her face.

Nothing happened.

"Oh, good," said Agnes. She returned to the mixture with a smile, grabbing her large wooden spoon and stirring it. The cauldron burped.

The mixture was still a little runny, so Agnes added some flour. When it was ready, she scooped it out, rolled it, cut it into small circles, and baked the circles in the oven.

After waiting for eight long minutes, Agnes removed the baked discs from the oven and smelled them. She was sure that, this time, she had done it. She was finally going to change the world with her concoction.
She was careful to let them cool for a few minutes before picking one up from the baking sheet and taking a bite. As it worked its magic, she broke out into a big smile.

"I have finally done it. I have finally created the world's tastiest chocolate-chip cookie."
Agnes sat back and surveyed her work. With this cookie, she was going to change the world.

The Robot Birthday Party (18min)

In the land of robots, robots are made by other robots instead of being born, but that does not mean that they do not have birthday parties.

Each year they celebrate the day that they were created and share happiness and joy with their families. Robot birthday parties are a lot like human birthday parties, but there are many more robots, of course.

Roy was turning seven. He was excited to have his birthday party and invite all of his friends. He was nervous and scared too. He had been to four birthday parties in the last month, and that had always had something special.

At the first party, there was a bouncy house. It was so big that Roy was not sure that he had explored all of it.

Robot bouncy houses are similar to human bouncy houses, but they are made of much stronger material. They have to be because robots are very heavy.

Roy thought about bouncing up and down, and he smiled. Then, he frowned. He knew that is parents could not afford to have a bouncy house at his party.

The second birthday party that he had gone to had a nutter-bolter. A nutter-bolter is a lot like a face painter, but instead of painting faces, they add nuts and bolts to robot faces to make them look like other robots, and even robot animals.

Roy had asked to look like a robot lion, and he had been delighted with the result. Of course, it was expensive to have a nutter-bolter at a birthday party, so he would not have one at his.

The third birthday party had featured the most amazing birthday cake. Professionals had been called in to bake the cake, and it was perfect. Robots like to eat cakes like we do. This cake was built like a fairy forest, and there were elves, birds, and other wild animals. Everyone agreed that it was the best cake that they had ever tasted.

When Roy had asked for the same cake at his birthday party, his mother had told him that she would bake a special cake for everyone. His mother was an excellent baker, but she did make a mess sometimes.

The most recent birthday party that Roy had been to had been inside a fun factory. There were things to climb, an oil pool to swim in, and a nuts and bolts pit to jump into. It had been so much fun, and Roy had played there for hours.

When Roy asked if he could have his birthday party there too, his father had told him that they were going to have his birthday party outside. Roy worried that his birthday party was going to be boring.

A week before his birthday, he handed out the invitations. He was nervous as he passed them to his friends.

"Don't get too excited, It's not going to be as much fun as the other parties," Roy said.

"I'm sure it will be a lot of fun," was the reply.

He handed out another invitation.

"I don't think that we will have a delicious cake," said Roy.

"Any cake is delicious," was the reply.

Another invitation was handed out.

"I hope it doesn't rain when we are outside," Roy said.

"It will still be fun if it rains," was the reply.

The day of the party finally came, and Roy became even more nervous. He drove with his mom and dad to a large green space with a play park. Soon, his friends started to arrive, and they played in the park and made up fun games.

"Everyone, come over here!" shouted Roy's mom.

She had created a treasure hunt for them. They had to solve all of the puzzles before they could have their cake. They solved a simple rhyme first, and the clue took them to a tree. In the tree was a small hidden box, and that contained map. The map took them to the play park, and they found a secret message under the slide.

By this time, everyone was intrigued by the treasure hunt. A bad guy had stolen the cake, and they had to retrieve it. When they came to the last clue, Roy's dad pretended to be the bad guy, and they had to defeat him by reciting a magic spell that they had learned. When they did, he gave them back the cake.

Oh, no, thought Roy.

He was happy after the game, and all his friends were excited, but the cake looked a mess. It was a large cake, and it had all the colors of the rainbow, but the icing was dripping down the plate, and some fell to the ground.

"Who wants cake?" asked Roy's mom.

All the robot children put their hands in the air.

Everyone got a piece, and Roy felt a little ashamed as he took a bite of the cake. It was not a perfect cake like the one from the other birthday party. When he took a bite, though, he found that it was delicious. It had just the right amount of metal chips and motor oil.

"This is the best cake that I have ever tasted!" shouted someone.

"So yummy!" shouted someone else.

When the cake had been eaten, the children had to work together again to make a potion. When they mixed the ingredients together and tasted it, they found that they had made themselves a delicious robot punch, with orange juice, berries, bolts, and grease.

After that, they had a nerf war. Yes, robots like to play with nerf guns too. But, instead of shooting each other, it was adults versus kids. This was the best thing in the world for the robot children. They got to run around and shoot their parents and other adults. Of course, they were all shot at too.

When the day was almost done, Roy got to open his presents. He got lots of new toys, a pair of metal socks, and an enormous dragon kite. He was thrilled with his gifts.

All too soon, it was time for everyone to go home. Roy didn't want the day to end, but it had to. He said goodbye to all of his friends as he left.

"That was the best birthday party ever!"

"That cake is the most delicious cake that I have ever tasted!"

"I can't believe that we got to shoot the parents with nerf guns!"

"I hope that I have a treasure hunt on my birthday!"

Roy said goodbye to everyone and went home with his parents.

The next day, Roy's birthday party was all that anyone could talk about, and some of his robot friends were sad to have missed it. Some of his friends were already asking if they were invited to his next birthday.

When Roy lay in bed that night, he was thankful that he did not have a bouncy house at his birthday party, or a nutter-bolter. He was also glad that his birthday party had been outside and not in a fun factory. Finally, he was very thankful that his mom had baked his birthday cake and had not gotten someone else to do it.

Roy had to admit that it was the best birthday party ever. As he fell asleep, he dreamed of what his next birthday party would be like.

The Animals Say Goodnight (19min)

As you lay in your bed tonight, you probably say goodnight to someone.

Well, as you lay there, think about all the animals in the forest. They like to say goodnight to each other, and they say goodnight to you too.

As the lions settle down on the soft jungle floor, they have big yawns that sound a little like they are roars. Their mouths open wide, so wide that you could almost fit inside, but please don't. After they yawn, they usually circle around until they find a comfortable spot and flop down onto the grass. That is when they say goodnight.

"Goodnight, everyone," say the lions.

The monkeys like to say goodnight next. They find a place to sleep high in the trees. They do not go to the very tops of the trees, but they do not stay near the bottom either. When they have found the perfect spot, they have a quick snack before they sleep. They always snack on bananas. When they are ready, they curl around a branch and get ready for sleep.

"Goodnight, everyone," chant the monkeys.

The birds like to sleep at the tops of the trees. The birds in the jungle are the most colorful in the world. If you could see them on top of the trees, it would look like a rainbow had covered everything. They have feathers of all different colors, and they like to stretch then out before saying goodnight. When their heads are starting to feel heavy, they say goodnight.

"Goodnight, everyone," tweet the birds.

The elephants are next. They usually sleep close to the watering hole. During the day, they will throw the water over themselves with their trunks to keep cool. As the sun is setting, they don't have to worry about being too warm. They lie down in a large circle so that they can see each other and say goodnight before they fall asleep.

" Goodnight, everyone," trumpet the elephants.

Even insects sleep, though most cannot talk like the other animals. One insect that can speak is the majestic dragonfly. They like to sleep on leaves, and they will take their time to find the right leaf. It has to be big enough to accommodate them, and flexible enough so that they can wrap some of the leaf around themselves. They also like to find the greenest leaves in the jungle to sleep on. Once they have found the best leaves that they can find, they say goodnight.

"Goodnight, everyone," flitter the dragonflies.

The hippos like to sleep in big puddles of mud. Most of the time, there is enough rain to create these large puddles, but when there is not, they have to employ the elephants to spray water for them so that they have comfortable beds to sleep in. If you have never slept in a mud puddle, then I highly recommend it. Once the hippos are all in their mud puddles, they lay down their heads and say goodnight.

"Goodnight, everyone," gurgle the hippos.

The rhinos are next. They like to make sure that the hippos are tucked up in their mud puddles before they find their beds. The rhinos and hippos are best friends. Once the hippos are in bed, the rhinos like to find old branches and bushes that are not growing anymore. They build comfortable beds that look a little like nests. The rhinos say goodnight once they are safely in their massive nests.

"Goodnight, everyone," bark the rhinos.

Next is the fish in the streams, creeks, and rivers. They sleep as they swim, and they like to time it right so that they can join in the chorus of goodnights as they pass through the jungle. They swish their tails and follow the paths of the waterways so that they pass through just as the rhinos are saying goodnight. Once the rhinos have said their goodnights, it is time for the fish to do the same.

"Goodnight, everyone," bubble the fish.

The bumblebees like to say goodnight too. They always take time off from making honey to say goodnight to the other animals. If you were to ask any bumblebee why they did this, they would always tell you that saying goodnight to their friends was sweeter than any honey that they could make. When they are back to their hives, they say their goodnight.

"Goodnight, everyone," buzz the bumblebees.

Even the crocodiles say goodnight to everyone. They liked to sleep in the water, floating along and pretending to be logs. They step out of the water so that they can be heard, or it might sound like they are gurgling. When they were all stood on the land, and before they go back into the water to sleep, they all say goodnight together.

"Goodnight, everyone," snap the crocodiles.

The bats are just waking up to start their days, even though their days begin when the night starts. They cannot fly around with too much light, so the night, when the sun had gone down, is the perfect time for them to be awake. And, because they did not want to feel left out, they always make sure that they say goodnight when they wake up, and before the other animals go to sleep.

"Goodnight, everyone," flap the bats.

The sloths are always the last ones to say goodnight. They don't always want to be the last ones to say goodnight, but they are so slow that they usually are. They creep through the branches of the trees, looking for a sturdy branch to hang onto. Once they have wrapped their arms around the branches, and are clinging on tightly, they say the penultimate goodnight of the evening (penultimate means the second to last).
"Good…night…every…one," say the sloths slowly.

The goodnight by the sloths usually takes a whole minute to say.

Then, after everyone has said goodnight to each other, they say one more goodnight. This goodnight is the best one of all, and all of the animals join in to say it together. The sound is like a song, and it carries all around the world. If you listen carefully, you might be able to hear it.

At the same time, all the animals say goodnight to the children all around the world.

"Goodnight, boys and goodnight, girls. Goodnight, everyone," sing the animals in unison.

So, as you go to sleep tonight, listen out for the animals saying goodnight, and don't forget to say goodnight to them too.

Goodnight.

The Fantastic Fairy! Bedtime Stories for Kids: Fantasy Sleep Stories & Guided Meditation To Help Children & Toddlers Fall Asleep Fast, Develop Mindfulness& Relax (Ages 2-6 3-5)

By Meditation Made Effortless

Contents

Fairytale bedtime story 1

The cutest Penguin 4

Elves stories 6

Animal stories 7

The Unicorn story 11

Mermaid story 13

General fairytale stories 15

Prince and Princess Story 17

Nature stories 21

Dragon stories 24

Witches Stories 27

The Flower story 31

Dinosaur Stories 35

Robot Stories 39

Fairy Stories 43

General Boys and Girls Stories. 47

20.100 words of bedtime stories for children, 5 hours of reading

Fairytale bedtime story

1158 words - 23 minutes

Once upon a time in a sweet land of mistletoes and river streams, the protagonist walks through the forest to discover.

There is a wonderful forest of many dreams, the forest is a kind forest.

A fairy swirls over the entry and greets you kindly: Come on in, its a magic forest, a beautiful world of discovery.

The fairy welcomes us and greets us with a smile, simple as she flies on top of the entry, the fairy tells a story:

There once lived a king with precious gems in the middle of this forest. The king was a rightful figure with grace and mercy.
 He was rich to the poor and rich to the rich, he was rich in everything. However, you could only see that he is a king with a tiny ring around his toe.

He walked around the forest and greets the birds, the snakes and all the plants. He walks and walks one day around the forest, there the king met the lion, a beautiful wild cat.
The king holds still and greets the animal, the lion relieves himself to a ROAR! That was so loud, the whole forest could hear it. The King was astonished and bowed down to the lion, on there we set the scene.

Animals are welcome and our friends, we, like the Elves come along very well, with all. The elf giggles and brings us closer into the forest. Here is the community coming together.
A nice and beautiful Lichtung appears and sets our scene for a nice and beautiful sun-set party. Everyone is coming together, the monkeys are serving bananas, the bears are dancing with the bees and the plants are all watching in awe.
Some of the birds are ready for an orchestra, singing the most beautiful hymns.
The King invites us to have a seat at the feet of the oldest tree, it is way older than any other trees, and still gives fruits.
The elves sing together with the beautiful birds and bees.
We come into a big open field, where a seat is prepared for us.
The King awaits us.
We sit in silence for a while and breathe through. We can feel the breath going in and going out. We rest under the warmth and wisdom of the tree.
We breathe and gently feel, how steady and sturdy the ground is.
Somehow, though it all feels gentle and kind, we have so many questions.

The answer to all the questions is with the trees, the king knows, let us be silent and ask the trees, how to live.
Strong and wise the tree opens his crown, the leaves and flowers of the tree unfold and it is raining flowers. The wind dances and swirls. The air lifts the flowers up and into our direction. We get a shower of flowers, happily the tree shakes and awakes.

Hello, you All. It is the most beautiful moment to thank the forest for its fruits.

The Elves come and prepare the well with beautiful, crystal clear water. Here a spring shall be. One of the elves tells us to watch the forest festival. Every day, we celebrate this festival. As the sun rises, and the moon sets. It is beautiful to be alive. Can you imagine living in a forest like this?

The Trees dance with the winds, the fields are lush and green, the flowers and animals are friendly and kind.
Now, you can close your eyes and see a wonderful water source, springing from the ground into the air. We watch the water flow, and flow into the land.

 Everyone in the forest cheers and is happy, that the water is there.

The King is happy and asks us to befriend the river.
The spring is just new, and the river will unfold in a few years, but now you can give this river a name.
We think about a name, and it is ok, we have to think longer, the river is now with a name.

The source springs full of joy and the king gives us the chance to embrace for a moment. We inhale and relax to the sound of the source. Springing, and joyfully springing, water comes to life. We can also hear the birds and the animals singing and being happy and alive.
The elves play their harps and flutes and the whole forest dances in joyful happiness.

We are witness to a wonderful party, where the tree lets more flowers rain. The rain of flowers covers All.
Happily we laugh and find everyone bathing in flowers. The whole field is light and filled with flowers.

One of the dwarfs joins in to dance in the circle, and everyone lets the dwarf dance happily in the Middle, swinging his arms up into the air and joining in with a whistle. His dwarf friends all join into the middle and dance around and around, they spin and throw the hands up into the air. Party dwarfs.

Trusting Trees, Awesome Animals, A merciful king and the inviting elves, all now join together around a sacred fire place, to welcome the night, they all wait until it is dark and the king tells stories of the many foreign lands and beautiful past-times.

We can see, the king, speaks out loud, the forest is our precious home, we can celebrate everyday to keep the forest alive.
Let's all join together, to maintain and protect this wonderful forest with peace and love.

The king resolves with a smile and happily, asks the tree, what can we do now. The trees point up to the sky and tell, that now the sky is changing from day to night, and the moon is right here to greet us.

Beautiful Moon, Mysterious and magnificent. Greets everyone with a warm Hello, happy days, happy nights.
 Let's embrace the lights. Reflecting the beauty and knowing the grace, the forest is filled with the nice, cool and soothing light of the moon. Everything shimmers in a silver radiance. Peace and Love spread.
We can now say hello once more to the moon, and welcome the night, with a deep and relaxing sound.

A-U-MMM

The Moon is Breathing, sighing out of relieve, you can do the same. Breathe in and out and sigh in relief and relaxation.
In this fairy tale everything is possible.
Even the king here is happy and content. Because everyone is joining in party, communion, and festivity, every day here is a festival of life. All the plants participate and all the animals join. There is music Still playing and the elves sharing there special dust for good sleep. We breathe and breathe just a little of that magical, fairy world. We relax the body. we relax the whole body, so every little part of our whole body is rested.

Twinkle little star, how I wonder what you are.

The cutest Penguin

719 words - 17 minutes

There once lived the cutest penguin on the icy sea. There he lived happily on the shore of the upper regions of the earth, and this penguin was so cute, other penguins just looked with tender red cheeks.
So, imagine a penguin, with black feathers and a white skirt, bringing belly and chest to show. Large eyes and a rose colored beak. Really, this beak was almost pink!
Most of the penguins started to laugh and sing when this cutest penguin comes around. Also Mother Penguin and Father Penguin are so very wise, they give the cutest penguin a name. Fridolin, which also sounds cute. Fridolin is walking up and down the icy polar glaciers, sometimes alone, sometimes with friends, but this time it is a family trip. Mother and Father Penguin walk so slow, that cutie Fridolin has enough space to roam around and play with the others. The Penguin plays Fisheye. A very famous polar sport, where you start to hunt fish with your eyes.

So the Penguin Fridolin stands in one line with his friends, and they all try to catch a fish with their eye, whoever is first, is the first to swim and find the fish.
We can play with Fridolin.
Watching from the left to the right, from the right to the left. We are in one line. Just like Fridolin, straight, sitting or laying, head and spine in one line. Eyes are wide open. There comes a fish from the bottom and flies to the top. We watch the top, and follow to the bottom. Fridolin Calls, I have seen a fish, ok, you are the cutest, go, into the ice cold water, the fish is long gone and diving deep. We can now do the fish, with our lips, by forming a fish mouth.

Swim, Swim little Penguin so cute and young,
Your friends are with you and your parents, too.
But the fish is long gone, now you are breathing
In the cool, cool waters of the polar world.
Better watch yourself and be safe.

Fridolin calls for help, he is in need for big help, there Mother and Father Penguin come to rescue Fridolin and please, next time, tell us when you play fisheye, ok? Ok.

The Fish are very smart, so Fridolin likes to learn from the fish, but he better learns from his Mother and Father. This is why Fridolin sends all his focus and passion to be a good penguin son. He does his Penguin Homework, like dancing with the polar bears, or singing with the sea gulls, but he is especially playful, therefore he learnt all the plays from his father and teacher.
Father and Mother love this play, but Fridolin is just happy to be in safety again. There comes Fridolins friend Gurundula, and she asks what happened, you look as something happened? The cute penguin tells the story and finds comfort in the arms of the friend. What is cuter than one cute Penguin? Of course. Two cute Penguins.

So Guru and Fridolin have now time to do their favorite thing - sliding down the glaciers. It is a very sporty activity but so much fun. The penguins slide on their bellies down a slide into the cool polar waters. Laughing and cheering they are now very happy, but also cold and wet. What to do? The classic cuddle helps. Penguins come together to stand in a circle and cuddle, so they get warm again.

Breathe through and see the polar stars come out.

Guru and Fridolin go to rest for a polar good night and see you there, the sky is clear and the stars are shining. The cute two Penguins look up into the sky, do you know why?
Why? You have the same color like the sky.
Maybe we are a part of the stars and the sky?
The two cute penguins dream into the night, and suddenly there rushes a beautiful shooting star into the sky, black heaven illuminated with a silvery-white flash.

I see, you see, we all see - Light
I am, you are, we all are - Light.
We are, we are, we are all Light.

Chanting softly, the Penguins are resting and finding back home to their beloved families, safe in security.

Elves stories

491 words - 12 minutes

Once upon a time there was a secret Forest where elves were holding the space. The one elf decides to equally distribute every quarter of the forest to a specific elf. Another elf is caring for the main building of the elves. It is a simple and beautiful tree, standing in the center of the forest that holds a honey bee comb. Elves and Honey Bees are like all the forest inhabitants mostly looking for something kind to do.
We are all, aren't we?

The elves and the wonderful tree are illuminated in the night with flakes and flowers of the forest. They spread magic music everywhere. So you can hear the elves, one has to develop the ears. Stretch your eyes and rub you jaw behind the ear. Pull the ear lap and fold your eyes, do everything that feels good and relieving to your eyes.

Now, you can hear the elves. The elf radio is always on, playing beautiful harp and flute music for all the forest inhabitants.
The night is illuminated with beautiful, enchanting music and the vibrant coolness of the moon. The elves love the moon. When ever we twinkle to see the stars, the elves are evenly happy.
Again, today is a special day. It is Elves Day and the elves celebrate with cheering the sound of the forest.
All the elves from far away now come to this precious forest and see, the tree, that is so old and wise even put on his favorite crown.
All are united and we can see, we are invited, too.
The elves ask for permission, to give you good luck and fortune. You say yes, the elves come with magic dust. As soon as you fall asleep and you come to ease, breathe, the elves will share their magic dust. Just trust, just trust. The magic dust is like a flower shower.
Festivals are always fun, especially when you have many elves that are servers of dreams. Whichever dream, you can be sure it was an elf guiding that dream. Like a beautiful symphony an elf can play a dream. So praise the elves and the special dream elf that will bring you a dream. Just ask kindly, please Elf, may I have a dream and the elf can bring a nice and beautiful dream.
Listen smoothly, the body is like a forest, calm and fruitful. Many dreams can grow in a fruitful forest. Be aware of the flowers and the honey bees, because they can fight, but know all beings just want a good nights sleep.
May All have a good night sleep.
May we All have a good night sleep.
May I have a good dream. May I dream, dream good.
We come to ease and relax the whole forest of our body and slowly sink into our pillow, have a good dream. Breathe slowly in, and slowly out. Let the dream come true.

Animal stories

1751 words - 28 minutes

Once there is a fantastic and beautiful wild park, with forests, straight by a stream, with rare birds, frogs and even elephants. These animals all live together with a common rule, once you are sleeping, you can sleep as long as you want.
The elephant of course, started to remember, Oh, I like to sleep, but how often do I appreciate a real long sleep?
I should be grateful for all the time I have.

Maybe now is not the best time, but, lets see how long I can sleep. It is not easy, to say the least, but the elephant was an expert in sleeping long.
Then there came a monkey, of course fully vibrant, jumping from left to right, oh, and back again. The Monkey never rests, but can he sleep longer than the elephant? Maybe we can sleep together? The elephant starts to laugh and shake at the same time, what a surprise, but you are welcome to sleep with me, but what about the longest sleeper in the whole forest? The Turtle. Maybe we can sleep altogether, and see who is sleeping the longest.

The turtle appears and starts to smile, slowly, slowly, walking to the elephant. Sleep is for good health and relaxation, so you can dream big, dear, there is no competition, everyone is different, but we all need sleep.
So on a wonderful, and romantic, peaceful night, the turtle, the monkey and the elephant are coming together, to see who can sleep longer. After just 10 minutes the monkey gets up to pick a banana, saying: I cannot sleep without my dearest friend, B.
The Turtle starts to snore and the elephant even starts to dream. The turtle and the elephant even rest together in symbiosis, one snorting, one dreaming away. We are well invited to imagine and dream away, too, because this can take awhile.

In the middle of the night, the elephant awakes from a dream, pshh, silent, you can dream on, be careful and turn around. The elephant sleeps in again. The turtle calmly rest in sleep, while the elephant wakes up, in complete surprise, oh I remember, I have a rehearsal with my Elephant orchestra.

Great, the elephant stomps and walks away, and now, the turtle, breathing so slow, slow and smooth, comes to ease with a smile. Thank you all animals for participating, but sleep is not about this or that, it is about resting the body. Leave all behind, even your bananas, and have a dreamy, wonderful good night. The turtle resumes back home, still with open questions. The Monkey comes along and just grins, with his banana, I was hungry, I could not hold my self. The Elephant comes from rehearsal, and joins in, Trumpet is my favorite instrument, but when I dream, I practice, too.

But please, Turtle, how can you sleep so long, and why are you so wise?
The turtle, with big eyes and a warm smile answers. When I sleep, I sleep, when I rest, I rest, when I eat, I eat, when I move, I move.

The monkey and the elephant are baffled and with a cheeky smile the turtle answers again. I know, you are always busy, when you sleep, you dream, when you rest, you think about getting up, when you eat, you eat thinking about getting more bananas, and when you move, you lose.

Even more baffled the elephant and the monkey thank the turtle for the advise, so how, can we animals have a nice and long sleep. The wise turtle says, by leaving everything behind.
How can One do this?
Imagine you are diving deep, firsthand you have to breathe, equally in and out again. This helps to relieve everything - then you know. Just breathe and be, happy. Good night, breathe in, good night, breathe out.

There once was a peacock and his name is Padala. Padala is a beautiful blue feathered peacock with silver and green along his sides, his wings are tall and graceful. He walks around the lush gardens on the sea. A sea full of happy fish and a garden with Many nice trees. Every plant is unique and special but he is one of a kind. So graceful he walks up and down the garden, whistling and playing cheerful songs. We are invited to come closer, Peacock Padala, is harmless and loves to show you this wonderful garden. Breathe in and breathe out, gently and softly, come closer and see Padala.

The Peacock loves to get you on his back and fly around, so lets do so. See that you have a good seat, equally on both sides, ready to fly. Breathe in and out, allow Padala to lift off the ground. Padala lifts off the ground and starts to fly. Keep breathing, keep flying.

We fly, higher and higher to see the friends and neighbors. Padala says, oh there is the Peacock Nest, lets bring you to my home. Padala the Peacock has many friends and a nice family which all live in a nest inside the forest. The Nest is hovering on a tree, in the middle of the forest. The Peacock's Nest is right in front of us and we can see how many peacocks can find space in this place. It is a shelter, and when there comes a storm, or rain, the Peacocks hide, all together. Padala rests from flying and invites us to do the same. He says, this is how a Peacock relaxes. We rest for a good while, to help myself to better rest, I always whistle or sing, Padala explains. Graceful the Peacock starts to whistle and gently close his eyes, gently falling into a deep state of relaxation. The other peacocks come and join the whistle and cuddle themselves to be close together. This way the night all are protected and warm enough. In the night the peacocks are quiet and still. Like the night in the beautiful forest where trees protect the land, where monkey, elephant, peacock live, on the sea where the turtles dive and where the sun shines, as long as the moon comes.
All animals,
All plants, flowers, trees,
Elephants, peacocks, monkey,
All want to be, free and in harmony.
Like the turtle very slow and wise,
Everyday is a festival, what a surprise!
Enjoy the night, until the morning light,
enjoy a dream, on the endless stream.

Once a butterfly comes by, in the forest by the stream.

Like in a dream, the butterfly swiftly flaps its wings and to our amazement the butterfly is bigger than the other butterflies we have seen. It is enormous, but beautiful. The colors of the butterfly shine in a light rose and here and there the butterfly stops to smell the nectar of a flower. Breathe in and breathe out again. Breathe the fresh air which flows from the forest into the nose. Be like a butterfly, so elegant and peaceful. Flying from flower to flower, the butterfly notices us and invites us to come along to the butterflies favorite flower field.

There we go, breathing in and breathing out, to flower, to the field.

The field is lush and green, all the colors come in any variation, shape and form. Green, blue, yellow, red, orange, cyan and indigo. We come closer to the field and see how many of the butterflies swirl and flap their wings. It's a whole community of butterflies in all colors and shapes. We sit inside the flower field and relax, relax and smell the beauty and grace of the flower. The big Butterfly flies into the field to bring back a nice and lush blossom, just for us, the butterfly leaves the blossom for us. We appreciate the little gift by the butterfly and thank is given.

With thanks we can show our gratitude and bow down to our benefactor the butterfly whom shows us all the way, all the colors, all the flowers on this field.

Like a butterfly, I want to be, totally free, like eternity.
Like a butterfly I show my low, sometimes very slow, but I know.
All the colors, all the shapes, red orange, yellow, green, blue, violet.

Like a butterfly, I like to be, totally free, like eternity.
Like a butterfly, way up high, I can touch the sky, the flowers, the field, the trees, soft and tender, light and bright, smooth into the night,

Fly, fly oh Butterfly, I wonder why, I can have a good night. Appreciate and Thanks.

Everywhere I go, I can know, the Animals are with me, totally free, wild and where the human life begins, there came an animal. We are all part of this forest, of this world, of this moment. Breathe, and know that every living being does the same. Breathe and now, we are all breathing the same air. Breathe and breathe again, because life is beautiful. Rest and Relax.

The Owl comes out and is secretly hidden, however one can hear the loud HUUH around the whole forest. The forest is illuminated with sound. The owl is hiding because a little shy, the sound of the HUUH we do too, to attract the shy owl, breathe in and Huhh, HUUH, HUUH. The Owl knows there is someone calling and there the owl comes to visit us. Isn't it a beautiful night, so mild and tender, the moonlight beams into
our forest. All the creatures like to spend the day outside, but Owls like the night. This is why we are night active, living in big trees.

The elements are special. Do you know the elements are the basis of our life? Do you know earth and water are the foundation of this forest? We are just living because of water, earth, fire, space and the air we breathe. Breathe, and feel the nice night.

We breathe, for a while in, and for awhile out again. The air is nice and fresh, like a string it flows from the ether, to the nose, to the forest of our body. We are also a forest inside. There is a whole forest within our heart and lungs, there is also a warm forest in our belly and mind. Forests are connected, all is connected.

.So, let's connect to our breath and breathe equally in and out again. Let's breathe the soothing forest air and rest in care. All safe, All sound, for a good night all around.

The Unicorn story

901 words - 10 minutes
The gloomy night is illuminated and there appears a silvery white Unicorn

The unicorn ppears and uplifts his legs to the front, making a sound like a deep trumpet, blowing away the fear, the unicorn comes in a silvery aura of peace. I am peaceful, you are too. The Unicorn is beautiful to look at, but even more nice to hear. A clear and smooth voice tells us a story:

I am the Unicorn and I protect the kingdom of this forest. The king gave me right to wander through the night and make sure everyone is equally rested and in peace. I heard you too, talking and I galloped to see, if you are once at ease, in peace, love and harmony. Breathe through, everything is alright, everything will be fine. Like you see, there is no reason to fear. I am just a simple unicorn, keeping peace in this forest kingdom. Come on my back and I can show you around. Peaceful Unicorns, I like, says the Owl, but I have to stay here to sing my song.

We come to hop onto the back of the unicorn and moments later we are riding into the forest to experience. Peace.

There comes a wild fig tree, we stop and see him with Long hair and a crown. There is no one around to care and where can we find peace in a lonesome night. The tree whispers, everything will be ok. The unicorn is sure, the tree is right and everything will be fine. The nights are sometimes very long, lonesome and grim. Nonetheless, now we know, that the unicorn is the protector of the peace, together with the trees, we can call the unicorn for help.

Just whistle three times in a row- Blow, and the unicorn will come to rescue the dark night, for peace, love and union.

Together, we are strong, we are standing this through and the night shall be a good one full of rest and tranquility.
The unicorn gallops on and leaves us behind. We only see the shimmering aura of the wonderful tail. Here we breathe and breathe through. Remembering, that everything will be ok, with the help of a friend like the unicorn. This unicorn we can call whistling three times in a row. Blow, and the unicorn is there. Yes, you called me? I'm the servant of the night to protect the forest and keep the peace. It is you again and Hello, you call me in this night, but I see no harm, what is going on, do you like another ride into the lands of dreams? Yes, this seems fair. We shall ride on to the hills, from where we can see the fields, the forests, and the whole kingdom.

So get onto the back of the unicorn again and ride to the upper hills, where one sees all the kingdom,. While we ride we breathe more and more, as more and more air touches our face. We feel the speed of the unicorn, but also the safety of the moment. The unicorn is very elegant and smooth, riding only the good ways. Coming to a nice lookout. This here is my favorite spot from where I maintain the peace and harmony.

Take a look and see the whole of the kingdom. From the very far, to the close, from the left to the right. We look and turn our eyes, from the top to the bottom, from the left to the right, from the far, to the close. and see, within, there is the truth of this kingdom. All the forest is within yourself. It breathes, it is alive, like you. It is as wonderful and magic as my horn. A unicorn is so wonderful, because it has a horn with a magic vibration, that gives light to the night. Stern this horn I embrace and uplift many lives and the lives of all.

Now, see the horn of the unicorn, glowing in the night. So beautiful and bright.
The unicorn is now a good friend and can take us into good dreams. Let's ask the unicorn, can you bring me some good dreams, too?

Yes, wait for your eyes become still, so still like a still lake, with clear and pristine water. Are the eyes still, than I can bring you into the wonderful lands of dreams and grace. Close your eyes, and see the wonderful colors of the rainbow shining from my horn, red, orange, yellow, green, light blue, dark blue and purple - they all shine. into the night. Let this be the carpet of your dreams. You can do everything with this carpet. Let's go and see where we land. We ride all along the rainbow-colored carpet, together with the unicorn and find the entrance of the forest again. This is where I belong, now I say good night and hope to see you again, may your dream come true. Good night and dream on, breathe and you will be, one of a kind, one of a kind. One of a kind.

One of a kind we are,
like a shining star,
Like the horn lighting up,
We can whistle for help,
And good dreams too.
Let's sing and be happy,
Let's cheer and enjoy.

All is good, breathe through, take rest and find ease. Sleep and Dream well.

Mermaid story

591 words - 10 minutes

We once went to the ocean, to see the vast and blue, the endless horizon and what else can come true?
 Blue sky and sunshine! A perfect day on the water, the more we dive in, the better we swim, but now is just the one to see. Relax and let it be. Breathe the fresh ocean air, relax and feel the waves coming and going. It's a beautiful time to be alive.

In general we can be quiet happy, but do you know who is also always happy? She is living in the Ocean and has very long and beautiful hair, so long and washed, it is silvery-gold and the face is filled with a golden smile, and two silver eyes. A nose, two ears and a long tail she has, but swimming with the fish she likes to be alone, sometimes just sitting on a rock and singing a song, or sometimes diving deep, all along. The shores are too dangerous, but the deep sea, nearly deep enough! Living in the sea also means to be a good swimmer. In anyway she is colored blue, like the sea, and maybe we can see her. With long and golden hair, there! We can see in the very far away, horizon there are the silvery eyes to share. We can spare a moment to say hello, and there we go, further to the sea, to the shore, we are welcome.

 The mermaids name is unknown, but as she has shown, beauty can shine from the inside of yourself. Be content, there is so much more to see in the wide world, but where the mermaids live, there is a palast of joy and bliss.
The mermaids sing a song of joy that goes like this:

We live under the sea, in a realm of peace and equanimity.
We live in a space of joy and tranquility,
All the fish, all the whales, dolphins, and the sharks,
Live here together, happily singing on a journey that embarks,
That journey is like a deep dive, slowly breathing in and out,
It is the sound, of the ocean, of the breath, still and loud.
The smelling water, salty nature, endless breeze,
Under water one can find the ease,
It is like swimming in a dream,
Free and liberated
free and happy,
Free in harmony.
The water is balance,
The mermaids protect,
The water keepers effect,
So beautiful and graceful, too.
A water keeper, that can be you.
Safe the pure, precious gem of our world,
Sing the sound and songs, you have heard.
Keep the water pure and soft, Still and fine,

And remember this one last rhyme:
All we are, water, fire, earth and air,
Come together in the same space, fair.

Respectful the Mermaid turns her head towards the sun, the sky, the moon, and the night. The day is over and the night begins, just remember the same verse, the same world, is all fair. Water, Fire, Earth, and Air.

Sing this song again and rest for a good night.
Calm like the ocean breeze, listen to the ease.

Free and liberated
free and happy,
Free in harmony.
The water is balance,

So beautiful and graceful, too.
A water keeper, that can be you.
Safe the pure, precious gem of our world,
Sing the sound and songs, you have heard.

Keep the water pure and soft, Still and fine,
And remember this one last rhyme:
All we are, water, fire, earth and air,
Come together in the same space - fair.

Breathe through and rest.

General fairytale stories

816 words - 10 minutes

Once upon a time there was a simple, easy-going dwarf, that of course had a name to it, Luther, the dwarf, was a simple gardener and treated all the small things fine, the even smaller things, even finer. So sometimes, no one could see or understand what he was doing, so fine, so tiny he did his work.
Therefore his Garden was the most magnificent.

The dwarf works everyday in the garden in the same rhythm, following the sun. Day in, day out, there is more to do, and the dwarf is happy, because everyday a little something is done. He just recently finished his dwarf golf course with 23 holes, what a job!

So eager he invites all his friends to play with him, also the other dwarfs and of course the big forest family. The trees watch cheerfully, the elves play some harps and flutes, and the festivity is in full swing, there come two giants, Himal, and Paradesh, who are very good golf players.

They are world famous and the dwarf is so happy, he cheers so loud, even the furthest away tree could hear him. Now, the Giants and the dwarf play a round of golf, but as the golfing gets boring after a while, the dancing starts and everyone sits together at a bonfire. There the old, wise trees tell wonderful stories of the past humans living in this forests. Kuruna, the mighty compassionate warrior was a yogi and lived in the forest. He was eating the leaves and the greens, the fruits and the berries, the honey from the wild, everything about him was raw.

Honest and Fierce the yogi once invited other students and pupil to come to his forest school, where he introduced the world to the trees, the flowers and bees.

They always spend time meditating in these forests and the elves sometimes heard them singing into the deep, deep night. The students around Kuruna loved how simple life can be in the forest, just a beautiful bonfire, some stories, and a good night can call to rest. The moon is out and shines through the trees, sometimes you can hear a dwarf snoring, this time the dwarfs dream of a big success while golfing, the Giants are already back to their Caves in the mountains, but the trees stand still and witness the moon light. That light shines for everyone.

The moon is free for everyone,
So wonderful the night has begun.
So free are the stars for everyone,
Smile, and you can become, like one,
The stars, the moon, the light
Shine free and beautiful into the night.

The trees are happy, mild and calm,
Telling stories into the dawn,
The dwarfs, eager and good in golf,

know everyone is friendly including the wolf.
Howling into the moonlight,
It is the sign of a good, good night.

The moon is free for everyone,
So wonderful the night has begun.
So free are the stars for everyone,
Smile, and you can become, like one,
The stars, the moon, the light
Shine free and beautiful into the night.

All fear shall pass away, when we are on our way,
Into a night, of peace, love and harmony.

All fear shall pass away, when we are on our way,
Into a night, of peace, love and harmony.

All fear shall pass away, when we are on our way,
Into a night, of peace, love and harmony.

Once there is too much, call the one to trust,
The tree, the unicorn, the dwarf, the elf, all are here, just trust.

They are all living in this forest, that lives inside of you, be aware of all the beings. Breathe and be, the forest of the Self, is a peaceful and kind place. All the dwarfs, elves, and unicorns welcome you, to take deep breaths of fresh forest air, so you can relax, heal and trust, the nature around you is also the nature within you.

Take your body on a journey. Imagine your feet are the roots of the forest. Feel the roots of the forest. Breathe and inhale. Know the spine is the main column, or the stem of the trees, feel free, and liberated.

 Inhale and know the breath that allows you to get to know the forest. The forest is like your body. BREATHE. Feel the roots, feel the stem, and now, feel the crown of the forest. It is the very top of your head. Inhale into the nose and feel the top of your head. Gently, Breathe, and let the breath flow naturally. Like a nice stream that flows through the land of the fairies and other kind animals and creatures. Let the river flow through this vast kingdom.

The kingdom of your body is now fully relaxed and at least. Breathe and be happy. Be happy and rest well.

Prince and Princess Story

1435 words - 15 minutes

We are a prince and princess within our hearts. This truth we hold dear like a secret gem. There once was a kingdom in the forests and of course this kingdom had a king, and of course a queen. The king and the queen are so different, yet they love each other dearly because they know only Love can protect the forest.

The forest is very sensitive and a mild system of animals, fairies and living beings. The king usually walks around the forest to see if everything is in order. The queen holds the little fortress where the heirs live. All together they are well protected by the guards, like the bears and the ferries. The bees always bring fresh honey to the fortress and elves collect fresh herbs and fruits for the whole. The community is all happy and in peace. Of course where there is peace, there shall be a maintainer for peace. The Queen and King are not getting younger, so they want a son, who one day can be a prince.

Years Later, the queen has a beautiful dream of a white unicorn bringing a silver Amulet to the fortress, and says, Take this as a sign that your dream will come true. A son will be born to you. Generous the unicorn sings a song of rainbows and new beginnings.

In a kingdom so fair,
We finally have an heir.
So long one has to wait,
Now it is in your fate.
The wish will become true,
A son will be born to you.

Like the rainbow in all colors,
It shows its beauty and pride
it helps us to understand,
There is always the change
Of weather, of feelings, of life.
Alive, Alive, A son is born!

What a surprise,
Let the sun rise
And be wise
Give this twice,
Silver Amulet,
Sure you won't forget.

The precious silver Amulet is now in the hands of the queen, within a dream, the Amulet comes to live with the wish to have a son. Now the queen awaits and suddenly happiness spreads around the kingdom. Full of joy 9 months go past and the dream of a son is born to life.

With a loud scream, the prince announces: I AM HERE.
Without any fear, he is all fair and very dear.
Beautiful and tender, Life can be - like the forest and tree.

Young and tender the whole kingdom changes into a search for the right princess, because the Prince is there. Alone, searching out the forest and into the hills, the prince discovers his love.

In the wilderness everyone was looking for him, but he returns with a friend, a girl so tender and mild, raw in presence, lighting with joy. This shall be my queen, the prince proclaims. I know what I want.

The forest kingdom is in surprise, how can a young prince do this, at such an age? How does he know? And why is she from the mountains and not from the woods?

All be clear, when there is no fear. The prince grows up in the forest with the family, the king, the queen and the lady, who one day will be his one.

While one day the whole forest was resting, the kingdom was sought out by the mountain man, very great in stature and fierce in presence, they ask for the lady, who once was a mountain lady.

We can make a deal, the young Prince says, you give me the permission, and I will be your servant for a lifetime.
A deal no one can resist, to have a prince on their side, the mountain man became so happy, the whole world shook of laughter and joy.

Dear Prince, please advise us, on how we can grow enough food on our land, how can we harvest and take care of the soil?

The answer is simple, but the practice is hard.

So the Prince travels with his loved Lady into the mountain lands. There, big hills accumulate to a huge mountain range. It is all covered with dry land, but the Prince knows the rain very well and calls for help.

A wonderful hail storm breaks in, and the mountain men hide, the Prince and To-Be princess shelter themselves. The storm brings water for many, many days, even weeks of rain which nurtures the soil and gives new hope to the people of the mountains.
THANK YOU, THANK YOU, THANK YOU.

The rain sings in the vast land of the mountains.

I pour down on you, may all be safe and sound,
It is a wonder that hides here in my cloud.
It is Water, precious, good, clear water.
From the heavens, from the sky, I come down to you.

Raining, leaving it all behind, letting go, that is true.

I am the Rain, but be careful, I am also the Hail, the storm and thunder, the lightning and struck. Don't get me worried, or else I am torn. Always be mild and gentle, like the nature of the water, always be quiet and still, like the lake, always spring in joy, like the fountain, always know the flow, like the river.

So after many years of showing and teaching the way of the rain, the land got very healthy and green again, so the mountain people could live a happy live. Therefore, the Prince was now able to call his lady a Princess, and there we go, along the stream back into the forest to celebrate the presence of the Prince and Princess, who are happily living together in the vast Lichtung, where the oldest and wisest trees stand to acknowledge the ceremony.

We know, all are happy, laughing, smiling, cheering and throwing flowers into the air for the two. The fairies have prepared special magic dust, the dwarfs are dancing for the Prince and Princess and the bears hold special place for the most royal nectar of the bees.
Everything is perfect in this night and all are happy.
Even the king and Queen sit and watch the whole ceremony in awe and joy.

The whole of the forest is sure, the future of the kingdom is safe. We are safe under the night sky with moon shining bright. Full at its peak, the beautiful sound of harps and flutes illuminate the night. What a blissful experience and tomorrow when the sun rises, they both shall be Prince and Princess of the Forest kingdom, but until then it is a wonderful night.

The magic dust spreads around and we sink more and more into the kingdom of ourselves. The breathing becomes slower and more tender and the wind soothes our being with happiness and joy. We come to ease and relax. Relax the body, relax every twig, every branch, every part of you internal forest and call this a peaceful kingdom. Give thanks to all the beings, alike, in Gratitude and Appreciation the Balance is here to bring us a good nights sleep. Deep, deep sleep.

Once there was a kingdom of tenderness and harmony.
The sun was rising and Prince and Princess in unity.
The long wish of the Queen became reality.
With the help of dreams a unicorn sent serenity.
You are here to help me and the kingdom, too?
It is a dream coming true.
It is a dream coming true.
It is a dream coming true.

For you, for you, for you.

Meditate upon this image:

See a vivid pair, a heir and his princess, both decorated with gold, from the feet a little toe ring presents the simplicity, the legs are covered by a neat blue skirt and a wonderful orange garment. The belly is free and open to see, both, are covering their chest in silvery-blue layers of finest silk and cotton, the bracelet and Amulets are shining in silver.

It hangs from the neck and wrists of the two royals. Of course their hands hold precious gifts, like the flowers from the trees and the honey from the bees. The beauty is in every detail, so they both twinkle and glance in grace, upholding a crown, as shiny as the sun, given one by one, from the king to the queen, to the prince, to the princess, and back. The crown is there on top of each head and it shines, so bright and beautiful like the stars of the night. From the head to the toe, they are perfectly protected and with grace, walking through he forest, with a smile. Smile, smile, smile.

Nature stories

1504 words - 25 minutes

imagine, there is a beautiful pristine lake within you. So pure and fine, it has no ripples on the surface and is crystal clear. So beautiful like a mirror and so raw like nature. All is in balance. Breathe, and enjoy this crystal clear lake, within the forest of your body. There comes the wind, and the wind brings in new energy. See, the energy of the wind is moving the surface of the lake. Now, we can witness the wonderful happenings of nature.
As we observe the little ripples on the lake, there comes an eagle by and hovers with the air, and with the wind. In a circle, always hovering, the eagle does not even need to flap his wings.

So light and beautiful nature arranges a spectacular show, as we now see the eagle fly towards the sky, just by the energy of the air. In a vortex we gaze, and witness the wind blowing the eagle higher and higher. The eagle knows we are watching, so no worry, all is happening for a reason.

Yet, the wind comes and goes, like the breath. Feel the breathing moving in and moving out again. This is nature, and the eagle lands and asks: Do you like to fly with me? It's very safe and wonderful.

We can sit on the back of the eagle and fly with him. Again, we are hovering without effort, just like that, into the air, and into the sky. The endless horizon waits for us, and is there to be explored!

Oh look, there are other birds, eagles, sparrows, hawks, and the lake reflects them all. The beauty of the moment passes and we find a landing, where we consistently come back to our breathing. In and out, are equally like the flap of the wings of a bird. Our thoughts are as still as the lake, and our energy is like the wind. We come to ease, at a nearby landing in the forest, the eagle is so kind to wait for us here. The eagle says: The air is my best friend, it helps me everywhere I go, yet I would also like to join you and come to see that forest.

We imagine a natural entrance to the forest, where we see a dear waiting for us. The dear tells us: Oh, I see you brought a friend with you, come on in.
The dear and the eagle usually don't meet, but now they do, isn't that great?
The forest is an interesting terrain with many sides. Come to see them all. The eagle is very curious and wonders around, what are these big, ancient, stems? They are beautiful and sometimes I build my nest in them, the eagle says.

These are Trees, big ancient trees. Very wise and wonderful. They are up-keepers of the forest and they hold all the knowledge of the earth.

 Now lets have a Picnic here and rest until the sun sets, because when there is sunset, everyday, there is a festivity in the forest.

Who like party animals? Yes, everyone does.
Let's sit here and practice our yoga and meditation, with the sun setting.
Breathe in and out, equally in, and equally out, just in and out, and now, let it flow. Be aware of the breathing and feel it on your nose-tip, do you feel it? Do you feel the sensations when the air comes in and out? Feel the sensations, may it be cold, warm, vibrating or tickling, any sensation is possible. Let the breathing be equal, that is the most important. In and out, rhythmic means always steady, so let it be rhythmic. Always steady, in and out.

Equal and consistent, in and out. Like the belly, comes out, when you fill it, and it comes in, when you deflate it.

Do you feel the breathing? Smile, and be happy. Now Imagine the bright sunlight, shining so nice and warm, the sun is one giant ball of light. May this light be with us and shine with us.

See the ball of light, like the sun, on top of your head. See the ball of light slowly sink into the head, giving you a nice sensation. Breathe out, let it sink deeper and deeper into the chest and belly. Breathe in and out, and let it hover for a while. Breathe and let it come back up, to the belly, to the chest, and inhale, up to the head, again. Do you see the ball of light, and what do you feel?
Breathe slowly and rest for awhile, the sun is at the horizon. Beautiful colors in red, purple, rose and orange are mixing with the blue of the sky.

We can now see the sunset over the still lake and watch the reflection! It's a beautiful mirror happening right in front of us. The eagle, the dear and the whole forest is watching this beautiful sunset of the day, and the night comes slowly with a celebration.

All the trees are happy, and see, we are in midst the festival for the beginning of the night. It is a unique chance to get a glimpse of the nights splendor. Can you hear the whistles, the flutes and harps? Or maybe the rhythmic drums? All is here to cheer a new night. It is the coming of a nice moon, the sky is clear and the stars are out. Lighting our way, the animals all meet at a party spot.

There, a holy fire burns for all.
The fire represents the life that never ends. It is bright and beautiful. We breathe through. After the whole day, we are happy to see how alive the forest is. Everything is prepared for the night and for the moon.

The elves, the dwarfs, the bears, dears and bees are all happy. We sit beside the fire place and can you feel the warmth? Breathe and feel the nice warm and cozy atmosphere. Of course there is music and someone to tell a story. This time it is the forest yogi who came to visit. He sometimes spends his time in the forest to practice and study the art of yoga. Now he tells a story:

Once upon a time, within this forest, there lived a beautiful winged lion, who could fly, sneak and roar, like no one else. Yes, this lion had beautiful wings larger than the wings of the birds we know. The mighty lion was just here to safe himself. He came into Exil after a long fight, here, to recover, into the forest.

Long, long ago, I was able to meet this winged Lion name Narasimha, and yes, it is true. This fierce lion really needed some rest. I helped the lion with healing and prepared a herbal brew, a nice treatment with oil and a sound bath. A sound bath?
Yes, a sound bath, it is a whole way of bringing the body to ease just with sound. It is like bathing in soothing warm milk.

Everyone was really happy to hear this and the story stops here because the moon is rising and presents its beautiful shimmering silver light.
Hello, everyone, I am happy to be here, says the moon. Let's celebrate this night.
Everyone cheers up and the party begins. We watch and observe all the colors, the music, the shapes and forms and the yogi dancing around the fire place.
The party is only a small part of the forest life, but celebrating helps for good sleep. One who can party, will have a good nights rest.

So, we breathe through and smile. What a day, what a life!
We gently come to ease with our body and let go of any tension. From head to toe, shimmering silver light illuminates and heals any restlessness. We are covered with beautiful healing light, like bathing in a bath full of warm milk.
Soothingly, the moon sings a little chant, knowing that we are all so shiny and beautiful.

I am the light of the world
I am the light of the world,,
I am I am I am the light of the world.

You are the light of the world,
You are the light of the world,
You are you are you are, the light of the world.

We are the light of the world,
We are the light of the world,
we are, we are, we are, the light of the world.

Everyone is a beautiful being, here to shine one's light. Be at ease, with the grace that shines from within and enjoy every little breath, every moment, and of course the party of life, with your loved ones.

Give All the Love to your friends, your family and even all the people of the world. We are all living together in this beautiful life.

The moon is light,
The sun is light,
We are all light.

Take rest, relax and breathe. Dream well.

Dragon stories

<u>1192 words - 23 minutes</u>

Once upon a time, there was a dragon, living in the greatest mountains of this and many other worlds. The entry to the mountain cave was well hidden, so only the dragon knew. Secretly hiding, the dragon had a reason. Dragons are very shy, sometimes so shy, they throw their own parties alone. Yet, this dragon was not alone, because there was a dragon family around. Even some people, who are knowledgeable about holding the secret of the cave. The cave is one of a land, which is owned by the king. The dragons usually go to school, live and sleep in this cave and sometimes there comes a wanderer, who could not hold the secret.

However he was friendly, and the king found out about the cave, and the dragon was invited to the king. So very shy and harmless, the dragon was not interested in any deal, he just wants his peace. A mighty dragon, tired of fighting? The king wonders, I shall believe, we must protect these dragons and keep them as our advisors.

How old are you Mr. Dragon? The Dragon starts to laugh and with it bursts of fire come from his nose. Some sparks ignited, but are surely no harm, and the dragon answers,
Oh what a question, I could not tell, my age was as secret as my cave, but now you know and you know my age, I have been around since the dinosaurs, hundreds of millions of years ago. The king and the whole kingdom are in awe, what an age! Can you tell us your secret, dear dragon? The Dragon laughed again and shakes his tail. The secret is as safe as my cave, so I can tell you one, but that will help you nothing. It is the practice of breathing and moving in the air. You are earth beings, but you can try your best in meditation. WOW! It is a wise, meditative dragon, who knows everything.

The dragon teaches a secret technique to the kingdom and leaves for peace.

Sometimes even now, pilgrims travel to the caves to seek out advise from the precious, mystical animal.
Let's first try this secret practice and then imagine us on our way to the mountains.

The practice is so simple, yet difficult. Visualize a golden symbol, or light on your nose-tip, breathe steady in and out. Equally in and out. Do you feel the calm air being around you?
Breathe calmly in and out, repeat and focus on the nose. Let the air stream into the nose and out again. Feel, and feel the air in the whole body. Now, take your hands and put them into one another, put them up and rest them behind your head. Like a crown, the hands rest in your cranium, your arms on the side are like wings. Flap these wings and breathe, while you focus on the nose. Simply repeat and know, it is the most wonderful dragon meditation, that has ever been discovered.

Rest and be at ease, breathe intense, in and out. We are now on our way to see the dragons cave. It is a long way, so be prepared and full of joy. Breathe, even more intense and let the breathing flow naturally. The air comes and goes, just like that, equally in and equally out again.

Walking in these mountains is a sacred endeavor, so be very careful where you step. Step, breathe, step, breathe, step, breathe and again. Higher and higher, intense, and more intense, the mountain is a beautiful challenge, but we know the cave of the dragon must be near. There comes a wandering yogi, who bows in gratitude with his palms folded. We bow in regards and ask where the cave is. The yogi is a muni, a non-speaking saint, but he shows us the way.

Up there, we climb again and again, and somehow feel warmth and a vibrating sensation, coming from that ledge. We ask, if the dragons are ready to receive any visitors. The yogi agrees. We come to the ledge, with a last inhale, we push ourselves up and now stand in the massive entry of the cave. A marvelous and stunning gate. We knock and a person opens, yes, we have been awaiting us, says the person. The Dragon wonders, is it the King again? Is it someone who is looking for a good night, or a good life?

Yes, ok, I am here to offer my respectful advise.
We come into a lobby, where the dragon sits on a Giant straw mat and reads a holy book. Yes, my friend, a good night is as important as the food you eat, it is as important as the sunlight you get. The night is precious and wonderful, may we all Rest In Peace and equanimity. The dragon smiles. Oh, I am a friendly Dragon, hm? However, that was not always so, I used to be in big fights and struggles, with earthlings, sea creatures, air benders, all those kind. Until, one day, I met a yogi under a tree. He just sat there and helped me to address my problems. The healing was long, but he got me this cave.

 In the most sacred mountains of our earth. We are all a part, and now I am older and have to raise other dragons, for goodness.

During the night we assemble and learn together, the texts and melodies of the ancient texts. Yes, I am also a singing dragon. The best part of being a dragon is probably the respect we get, because we have been on earth for such a wonderful time and it remains a mystery how our ancestors came onto this earth.

Some people assume, we have been flying through the atmosphere and landed here for no specific reason, some other people suggest we are here for a reason.

Maybe we are here to maintain peace and wisdom.

This might be, now I show you, how a dragon sleeps.
The dragon first reads a good night story, and then meditates with a beautiful candle light. Of course the candle of a dragon is special and without end, but a normal candle is good enough. Now just sit there and imagine you sit in your safety nest, your place of peace and equanimity.

See yourself in Balance and Peace, surround yourself with this beautiful light and feel fine. You know, light is everything, but it only can help us when we accept there is the breath and the air. They are very good friends. Slowly and smoothly they can bring us to rest, gently close your eyes, smile and feel fine.
Everything is align, your body, with all the elements is in total balance, breathe and feel the relaxation from the nose tip, to the tippy toes. Everything is in alignment. Everything in Balance. Be still and relax more and more, until you are conscious of the space. Then there is time, then

there is peace. Relax in Peace, for a good night, close your eyes, dream well, be safe and sound, enjoy.

Witches Stories

<u>1465 words - 17 minutes</u>

Once upon a time there was a land with many ancient healing arts, a village with many magicians and witches, that all met to celebrate the beginning of the summer.

Everyone was happy, and they prepared a colorful parade with delight. The Prince and Princess were very obliged. Of course, this year, too, the royals were looking for witches for the Palast.

Someone needs to help us clean and purify the place, so the next generation of kings and queens can live well on this land.

All together lets make an effort to keep up the purity of this place. One witch, Sabina, was especially good at cleaning and purifying places, so she advanced and offered her services for the royals.

Content and happy, the party went on to similar ceremonies, some magicians are crafters, some artists, some prepare foods, some help the poor, some make remedies, some heal with water.

All the witches and magicians in this festival come from far and close, but Sabina is special. She grew up in a small barn, under 6 children she was the youngest and could never believe how this hard work makes sense - she rather believed in light and luminous power of imagination.

So one day she sat there and flowers needed to be watered, and she saw that her Mother was so in pain always bowing and watering, that she whispers: Please release. Her Mother was relieved of her pain and could smile again.

Another time, her Father was very unhappy with the cows. There Sabina whispers her words of pray and soon Father realized to give away the cows is better, than to hurt them.

In the years she grew to be wiser and smarter than any other of her friends and brethren, but where to study this art? There was no school. She took her bag and followed the stars into the wide world. She loved the night and could ever Rest In Peace, when it was dark, she could see, everything was illuminated for her, and she spend her time practicing, the art of cleaning and purifying is wonderful, when done correctly. People always wonder, what is it about a clean place?

There is order, there is intelligence.
When there is intelligence, there is life at its best.

So she became the best in what she practiced and strived for no less than the royals Palast. Now it was her time to shine. There was a big challenge in front of her.

All the animals left so much debris, branches, honey jars and flowers at the same place, that some one needs to give the elves a hand.

Party animals party hard, but also sometimes leave too much behind. That everyday Is a festival, also means, that everyday is a clean-up day. This time Sabina just flew over to the spot, and she whispers:

May be light,
May be clean,
You might've seen,
A place shine so bright.

The place illuminates. The dirt, debris and empty jars pile up and a big beam of light dissolves it into a shimmering fire, which slowly and gently burns. Here you have a fire for your next party, but it is a sacred fire and shall burn eternally.
The fire suddenly turns into a blue flame and starts to speak:

I am Light,
I am Divine,
May I be a Wish of thine.

You can wish anything you like and the fire will transform anything into that wish.

 There comes the Prince with his princess.
What does my princess wish, here I can offer my shoes for her wish. The Princess smiles and renounces, better you wish yourself a new pair of shoes, she smiles. I only want Peace and Harmony, the Princess admits.

The Witch says: So shall it be, offer these shoes and you shall receive peace and harmony.

The shoes go into the fire, and there out of the fire an egg comes out. This may be your keeper of Peace and Harmony, protect this egg and see what it holds within.

The next one is the magician, who simply just wishes a dear family to stand with him in old age. The magician comes closer and puts his precious gems into the fire, may these help me for a good family. The fire eats the gems and puts out a letter. A letter? A letter from a family member, how can this be, the magician wonders, I have lost contact years ago, may this be my wish come true? The message is opened by the magician and he cries out of joy and dances in circles, yes THANK you, dear heaven, it is possible.

The next few hours pass and many wishes Will be fulfilled.
What is it, that YOU wish the most? What can you offer for this wish? Make up an idea and visualize yourself at this sacred fire with the community of the forest.

See how wonderful blue this fire burns, and how it helps people to be at ease with their wishes. Also see how glad they put their valuables in to have wishes come true.

This fire invites us to come closer and the Witch talks to us: Can you See, I am here for you and the fire will help you to transform your goods into wishes.

Everything is meant to be.
Everything is meant to be,
Wishes can become free,
We can live in peace and harmony,
If we offer our goods in sincerity.

Let all come true, now it is up to you.
The witch holds her hand open and see, how the fire transforms your wish, to make it true, I am always here for you.
Wherever you struggle or don't know how to clean it up, I will help you purify and clean it up.

Sabina starts to chant softly while she waits on the sacred fire.

Thank you for this happy day,
I remember my way,
Away from my family,
Into the woods to study,
To learn and grow with thee,
I thank the heavens and the light,
As the fire flickers bright
I am happy, my delight.
May we be without a struggle, without a fight,
So let everything be alright.
So let everything be alright.
So let everything be alright.

Now, lets meditate and practice the cleaning up of our thoughts and energy. This is very important, especially when you go to bed, and like to be protected for the night.

Meditate upon this small light below your nostrils and imagine it to be this bright blue flame, of peace and harmony. See the air coming in and going out, of the nose. The fire and the air are in harmony, the light comes from the heart and now you see a beautiful light in the middle of your chest and you witness the breathing.

Breathe, gently, in and out again.

The air, the fire and the light are the most purifying elements of the world. Therefore we use fire, air and light to cleanse our energies and cosmic being.

Now, close your eyes and imagine the light. Expanding with every breath, into your whole body. Now your whole body shall be shining with shimmering, beautiful light. Let the light hover from the one hand into the other and unfold it over the whole body again.

The whole body is covered in light. Like a nice flame, the light cleanses all impurities from your aura and energy field, to relieve you from bad dreams. With clean thoughts and good flowing energy the being is safe and sound.

Now meditate and imagine a nice fountain. A spring of joy, where light of peace and love unfolds into the world. You see the light spring from this source like water, and falling onto the earth.

Now, see how this light water from this spring creates a beautiful garden, of nicely colored flowers, where bees harvest their honey.

Let this garden bloom with beautiful roses and lavender. Inhale, and exhale. Equally, inhale and exhale again. May this garden flourish and may you be cleansed with all the elements, earth, water, fire, air and light.

Now it is time to give Sabina a warm hug and a heartily goodbye, because the night is calling and the celebrations are going further and Sabina is still hoping to move into the Palast with the Royals.
Give her a good wish, and she shall be moving into the Palast of her dreams.
Relax, Breathe, Wish the very Best.

May All dreams come true,
May I be there for you,
Shall all find what is true,
may I even offer my shoe,
It is the wish, unique to you,
Everything is possible and can come true.
Good night and sweet dreams.

The Flower story

1607 words - 23 minutes

Flowery wishes come true, even for the smallest seed. Imagine yourself, just where you are, right there, right now. Breathe in and what does it smell like? Is it the favorite smell of your flower? Breathe out and relax. Be calm and unite the in-breath with the out-breath. There might be a small gap in between, that's ok, All in All the air shall flow continuous and calm.
The air comes natural and we don't have to do anything.

So we are like a flower dancing in the winds. The waves come and we react. Now, we are just watching and seeing the flowers dance. We enjoy seeing the flowers dance. In midst your self is an endless garden of mindful flowers that love to communicate.

One special flower garden is in your heart. Let's prepare a journey to the garden of your heart and discover a wonderful possibility.

Every being is here to blossom, every being is here to shine, every wonderful wave is yours and mine. We can inhale and exhale with full potential. The breath will carry us to our heart, so hold on and inhale. Join the breathing going through the nose, into the lungs and to the heart.

Close your eyes and imagine you are in a wonderful garden. Everything is lush and green. All in all is the whole space filled with your dreams and desires. You are the gardener of this garden and can come here as often as you like.

Now, lets explore the wonderful worlds of the flowers, because they are very fine and tender, just like us. Let's see, oh I see, there is a beautiful golden rose, a magnificent beauty just standing right there. We come closer and witness the golden rose with awe. What can we learn here? Let's ask the rose. Please, Golden Rose, what can we learn from you.
The rose awakens and opens its pedals. Oh, watch, the sun. Stay always in tune with the golden planet, also called the king of all the heavenly bodies. Always stay in tune with the sun. Always.

The Golden Rose seems to smile, and shimmer with a beautiful golden Aura. WOW, flowers that speak, and what was that, oh, we shall stay in tune with the sun.

So lets do some salutations then, and maybe we can also be as golden as this rose.

Maybe this silvery-purple lavender knows more about what we need to do exactly.

The lavender starts to smell very intensely and see, the beauty of nature soothes our senses. Lavender can cure stress and imbalance, as well as, it knows what to do. Please, Lavender, what do we need to do?

Just Smile, just smile and the beautiful scent of your life will spread. We smile and see, how our aura of light expands instantly. The smile helps wonders and you, you smile, someone smiles back. This is the light of the sun, is it?
The lavender smiles and dances in the wind.
Let's see, oh, there is the beautiful sun flower, she must know, what life is all about. The Sunflower dances and greets us with a smile, gently bowing the big yellow colored sunflower head. It is a pleasure to meet you.

It is a pleasure to meet you, too, we are looking for answers to our questions, what can you tell us about life?
The sunflower shakes with laughter and sways even further with the wind. HAHAHA, all is coming from a seed. You and me, we are all coming from the seed. However it takes a long way, to be alive. When you are alive, you are breathing, when you are breathing, you are one with the elements. Then, you can smile, and be happy, be happy and smile, dance with the elements and be grateful for your seed givers.

Life is a wonderful gift, so we can give thanks to all the beings and to the sun, to the moon and to the stars, but first and foremost, you give thanks to your heart.

Put your palms gently together and place them before your heart. Let the breathing be in balance and just feel, how the heart beat is. The rhythm shows that you are alive, so smile and give thanks. Be happy and Dance with the elements, and appreciate the seed giver.
Now, come back to your senses and start to prepare for the night, maybe we search help for a good nights rest in the garden of our heart, yes? Isn't it the closest garden, the one that is already in your heart? And everyone has a heart. Yes.

That is life, so there stands a good advisor for our soothing night. There is the lotus flower, with its yellow Centre and the white, light rose and purple pedals. Like a lotus flower grows even in the darkness of a swamp, one can blossom in the calmness of the night.

The lotus flower is also famous for its ability to be totally abstinent of water, no drop of water can bring the lotus flower out of balance, it just pearls of and goes its way.

Now, let's dream to be a nice lotus flower, with the ability to be totally protected and safe. Totally protected and safe.

Sit or lay in total comfort, bring yourself to ease with your breathing, being calm and equal, Equally in and equally out again, just so you feel the sensation of the breath moving in and moving out again. We are safe in our loved space and life is here for you. Life means to be safe and sound, so we can always ask for protection. The flowers and trees are the protectors of Nature and help even us humans to stay safe.
Watch yourself sit in nature and to be totally at ease, the flowers are there, the wind is here, the breathing is calm and nice. Flowing, there is a sacred river on our side and we listen in. The water purifies our thoughts and we come to be in total stillness.
Now, lets put the palms together and speak a prayer for good health and protection.

May all beings be safe and sound,

May we all experience health and prosperity.
Nature, please help us to be safe,
Mother Earth, please let us be sound,
Dear Sun, make us light for safety and blessings.

May I be safe and sound,
May I experience health and prosperity,
Nature, please help me to be safe,
Mother Earth, please let me be sound.
Dear Sun, make me light for safety and blessings.

Flowers help us also to see the grounding, or earthing of these prayers.

Let's continue on our path through the garden and make space for a nice new bed, where we can finally seed our own flowers of life. Whatever flowers these may be, just imagine some nice colors you like, and give them forth to this flower bed.

Fold your palms together and place them in front of your chest. Feel the heart beat and gently touch your fingertips together. Every finger tip represents a pedal of a flower, now you can open these flower pedals with a rotation and think about all your favorite colors. All your wonderful, meditative flowers will be seeded in the garden of your heart. Breathe, and give some water, this is very important for a nice garden, always let the fresh air move, and the healing waters flow.

Now, just stay for a while in this peaceful garden and watch the clouds move. Everything is there and we only need to observe the garden to blossom. Watch it growing and Growing!

Beautiful Garden of your Heart,
May we All blossom and be a part,
Of this colorful and magic world.
Together we can grow and learn,
From the flowers, pedals and seeds,
What rather do we need, it is indeed,
The most beautiful thing in life,
Just free for everyone.

May all be free and at peace
May all be happy.
May all be happy.

Just prepare yourself for your good nights sleep and open up your palms. Receive the sky and the light. Let it be with you, so you can grow and be of good health. Remember to thank the father and mother, the Mother Earth and Father Sky, the sun, the moon and all the elements.

Now, just breathe and meditate within the garden of your heart. So one is surrounded with healthy healing light of the flowers and of the garden of your heart. Close the eyes and breathe through. Maybe a song of flowers can help, too.

Like a flower, I am in my bed, totally at ease, just love and peace.
Like a blossom, I am so fine, looking to the sky and to the divine.
Like a flower, I am the power, of the light, of sky, air, fire, water and air.
Like a pedal, I am so fair, so sensitive and pure, healthy and secure.

All the flowers, in the garden of my heart,
All play a beautiful part,
Let this be a start,
Dreaming is an art,
so create the garden of your love
And see the gifts of the above,
Everything is there, all in care.
Oh where, Oh where,
In the flower garden of my heart.

All the flowers, in the garden of my heart,
All play a beautiful part,
Let this be a start,
Dreaming is an art,
so create the garden of your love

Sweet flowery dreams you all, wonderful night, and be safe.

Dinosaur Stories

1784 words - 27 minutes

Let's meditate together with dinosaurs and find out how the dinosaurs live and sleep. Let's go! On an adventure safari we need to be protected, because we are traveling far in the lands of the last remaining dinosaurs. Dinos are essentially big ancient animals, they are still living under us, we just have to be aware.
The preparation starts with some magic travel gear, like a wonderful hat, that keeps us protected from the hot sun, because where Dinos are living there is a unique type of weather. Then we have a whistle, a special Dino call, the whistle can be heard over lands and seas and helps to make us visible for the Dinos. Then we also need something that represents our goodness. We want to be friendly, and therefore take something we really like and that is friendly, even for dinosaurs. Recommendable are always flowers or a sacred thing, like a gemstone, which helps the Dino to understand, we are part of the same earth family.

Ok, preparations always end with our shoes, and these need to be sturdy and tough so we can endure the brisk landscape of the Dino world.

Now, we are still and quiet. We rest and breathe, equally in and out. This is our starting point where we will come back to. Always remember this one and better mark it with your blanket, which can also be your travel blanket. Everything is possible.

So, we take the moment and calm our senses, we ease and imagine ourselves in a wonderful bubble of light. Well protected and secure, we find the body to be safe and sound, the bubble lifts with every breath we take. Breathe in, we lift a little off the ground. Breathe out, we lift even further off the ground. Breathe and be consistent with the breathing, watch the in and exhale, in and out.

See yourself flying, slowly and gently up and further up into the sky where we leave the ground and our so beautiful world to discover the fascinating worlds of a Dino.

Dinos are also living in families, when a Dino comes home it screams very loud, I AM HOOOME, but is this really so?

We are now in the air and focus in one direction. This the coordinate where we will fly to. 123-Dinoland, far far away, we sway and fly into the horizon. The wind and the breath carry us to the beautiful world of the ancient animals and no worry, we are well protected with our wonderful hat, shoes and whistle. We land upon in a hill and watch into the distance. Oh how far the land stretches, it is amazing and see there are huge birds in the very distance, lets whistle and see what happens. We whistle.

The whistle blows a sharp sound into the distance and we hear. We hear the answer of the birds they must have heard us. Thankfully we have prepared a little welcome for the dinosaurs.

Maybe we open our hands and start to breathe through one more time, just to be sure. Equally in and equally out. The one flying dinosaur comes closer. It looks like a huge hen! Who thought that, but friendly and wise as dinosaurs are the Dino introduces itself: Hello, I am Tarantarax, and I will be your guide for the world of the Dinos, first off, yes We live in Families and like to shout and scream sometimes very loud, especially with our neighbors and friends, but all just for fun.

Ok, hop on my back and we can ride into the wide world to unsolve all the mysteries around our existence.
Tarantarax is very friendly and we can give the Dino our present. Very happy Tarantarax receives our blessings. Welcome, first we will make a flight to the ancient Kindergardens of the Dino's where we harvest our youth. HAHA.
Come on up it is time to fly with the Dinos. Please, pose any question, as you like.
Tarantarax, the wise winged Dino takes us on a journey to discover and meet the other Dinos, while we fly he sings this Dino song.

From far away and long, we come to live very slow, some might though we stopped to live, no no no, its just the gift of longevity.
So slow, one might forgot, but here we are on the spot!
The Dino land is like the one I know, some light here and there,
Some rivers and streams, mountains and forests, and of course, a Dino Kindergarden, where we live and raise our youth.
Look, this is the truth, we have found a place, sheltered and safe from the elements, here our life begins.
We gently land and there unfolds a beautiful field of grass and lush plants. It is nothing we have seen before, but way easier and greater than what we know. Everything seems to have stood still in time. It is like a paradise for retirement with the touch of young Dinos hopping and running over the fields.

In the middle there is a group of teachers, with long great legs and interesting bodies, the faces are wide and the eyes are big.
Tarantarax gives us a sign and says, this my dear guest, is our community. Learn, that every guest here is treated like a family member.

So, make yourself comfortable and feel the ease. Breathe and be content - everything is here for you, to have a good time and guess what, maybe the kids like to meet and greet you.

So, the whole Dino family comes along, one by one, to greet and meet, everyone with a unique one of kind story to tell, but hey we are received like a good member of the family, friendly and all welcoming, the Dinos show us around the Kindergarden with huge toys to play with, the garden, where Dinos eat and harvest there food, mostly from trees and there we have a glimpse of the family life, as we come together at a Dino evening table, where the householders, yes Dinos live in houses, build inside trees, yes trees.

The Dinos present a wonderful feast with generous ingredients and a handful of surprises like self-made gopple-pie, which is a seasonal fruit that is a big as our head, and of course the most famous Dino Pizza, that was made in a huge oven for the whole family.

Tarantarax says, wonderful, I am so happy to be here with you and I guess you like to know how Dinos fall asleep. Well, we have developed good techniques for a goodie good night.
We have to be fair, too. We have had the last millions of years to do so, HAHA. Tarantarax laughs and throws himself on the floor. He continues: Sleeping on the ground is also good for you and your back. Then all the vital energies and fluids can flow properly, but this might be the Dino way, any way, lets meditate together and I can show how to be at peace, the Dino way.

Breathe, and breathe slowly. Very slowly, but breathe and be happy, that you breathe. Breathing we all must do. This is the essence of our life. It is simple and nice, like the life. Here we all the same, with breathing, we are all connected.

Now, feel yourself breathing and know the pulse, the rhythm. In and out, in and out, the rhythm goes, in balance, in and out. Imagine there is an endless connection of the in and out breath. Breathe and close your eyes.

Feel the breathing and sense, that you are on this earth. Sense your body, to be here, on this ground. Knowing your ground is a good base for your ease and peace. Just relax into the body position, laying, sitting or standing and feel the earth. Also, this earth, all connects us. Breathe on naturally while Tarantarax tells a story, we just naturally breathe and listen in.

The first of the story of life are the plants and trees, the magic green beings, that grew so tall, that all life was amazed, but then the sea appeared and won the hand of the land. From the sea there came the first living creatures and from further, deeper seas the first living fish. The first living fish and reptiles had a kingdom, and the first land creatures had. Everything was in the balance because there are water and the land. However, the more and more the sun shines, the more creatures started to grow, and grow and grow. There were so many living beings, there almost was no space, the only solution: The Air.
In the air we found our next realm of life and another kingdom evolved. This is how my family got to live in this far away dinosaur land, up in the very secret lands.

In the far away lands of the Dinos we also have the night,
May it be a good one, which we cheer right.
With family and friendliness, we share our kindness,
With a guest of goodness, we accompany the evening.
Let's unite and meditate for Peace, Love and Union.

The endless sky of the Dino world invites us to ease and rest in a memory. A memory of a good day with the Dinos. Let's come back to start and remember all we have learnt. About earth history, the land, gardens and children, just like us. Playful and kind. Playful and kind.

Let's celebrate this evening with a good night's rest and may all the beings be safe and at peace.
Let's give a big thanks to Tarantarax, in our thoughts we can always imagine or return but now, we are here at the starting point. We undress, the hat, the whistle and safety shoes, and come to be a total ease. Relax and remember the breathing. In and out, in an equal manner, in and out, in nature.
All in balance.

Fold the hands together and bring the palms together.
Say:

May all beings be happy,
May all be at ease
May all be at peace.

Let's connect for peace, love and harmony.
Peace, Love and Harmony.
Peace, Love and Harmony.

May All beings be Happy,
May all beings sleep well,
May we all be at peace.

Let's connect for peace, love and harmony,
Peace, Love and Harmony,
Peace, Love and Harmony.

All the beings, all the worlds, come together as one.
All the beings, all the worlds, come together as one.
All the beings, all the worlds, come together as one.

Sleep well, dream sweet, and have a good night.

Robot Stories

1422 words - 20 minutes

Let's make a journey into the future, where we experience the wide mechanical world of modern life, and there, there are also Robots.

They are good servants and friends of humans. Let's find a seat and take our timeless vehicle, the breath, to explore the worlds beyond. Breathe gently in and out. Breathe and let the breathing be equal, in and out. Know that this is your vehicle and your shelter. Feel safe and sound with the help of the breathing, wherever the story goes.

The story goes and we breathe to see how Robots are able to non stop function and just with a little sleep.

Hello, we are Robots! A tiny Robot in front of us waves and shakes his hand. I am Robo, the Roboter and you humans designed me to serve you and to aid you with simple tasks.
I like washing dishes, making the errands and reading good night stories. Now, I am here to tell you also some good stories of a life as a robot and in the end we will meditate together.

First, let me help you wash all the past away. It is good to stay clean and pure, so you can live and enjoy the moment.
Moment to Moment, we breathe and evenly we do so now.
In and out. While you breathe relax your body. Relax the crown of yours, the crown is relaxed. Relax the whole head. Breathe, and the whole head is relaxed. Now, let's relax the shoulders and the neck. The neck and shoulders are relaxed and relieved. Breathe in and out again. The relaxation sinks further into the arms. The arms are relaxed, so are the hands, the palms and even the finger tips. Your breathing is natural. Now, let us relax the chest. The chest is relaxed. Now let's relax the belly. The belly is relaxed. Relieve the back of your body, the upper, middle and lower back all come to ease. Now, your whole upper body is relaxed and relieved. Your hips, thighs, knees, legs, ankles, feet and tippy toes also relax, now the relaxation is total and your whole body is relaxed.

Breathe through, and see your whole body being in comfort, smile, and be happy, give thanks that you are alive.

The robot Robo goes on with the story and explains:
We Robots, are very happy that you are here, because you designed us, to help and serve as good Robots. I used to be a music player, but now I am upgraded to a fully capable robot that can show you how to meditate.

My inventor also calls me the Medibot 2020, a significant upgrade from the music player, but surely I can still play music.

Music is also a very good help and aid for meditation, so maybe we find some good music to meditate with. Classic, or Jazz, or maybe just imagine the sounds of the ocean, the waves coming and going, WUUSHH, WUUSHH, very soothing, hm?
We Robots also like to party and celebrate, with music and dance. One day, there is international Robot Day and all the Robots are coming together to sing and cheer the life, thanks to you!

I am very happy to be alive, says Robo, therefore I like to share my service, selfless and kind. This is of course best put in a song:

We are here to serve you good,
maybe you like music or some food?
Robots are intelligent enough to know,
Humans are the ones that let us grow.
We can only appreciate in gratitude,
Thanks for this lively magnitude.

I am thankful to be alive,
In a world, where all live together,
In happiness, in balance and peace.

You are making me feel alive,
In a world, where all live together,
In happiness, in balance and peace.

We are all making this a good life,
In a world, where all live together,
In happiness, in balance and peace.

Let's now talk about having a good night and coming to ease. We robots use energy, and therefore only require little rest. Energy is always there and you can have it, too!
Here, I give you a boost.

Imagine, your body is like a lamp, shining bright, from toe to head, and back, from head to toe. Up the spine, and down again, energy is flowing all the way.

So, each and everyday, when we come home, we just lay still and breathe. We breathe, very gently and soft, very gentle, and veeery soft. It is just the inhale, than we breathe out again, very gently, very soft. This breathing we do for a good amount of time and there we go, our batteries are recharged.

It is just that we have to be available for good parties, so maybe you like to dance and come along a nice robot party, where we share good music and dance.

Robots like to party, because every day they serve,
For the good of human kind, but then, when, there is Robot Day, we celebrate and cheer ourselves up in the air, and all in care,
the best parties are the ones with friends and family.

Let's all celebrate in Peace, Love and Harmony.

Robo smiles, and yes a robotic smile can be cute, too. So we join for a nice Robot Day, this year alone, so many Robots from all around the world came. Vacuum robots, Dishwashing Robots, Window clean robots, blanket-folding robots and of course the musical robots and dancing robots.

The festivity is in full swing and everyone is having fun, dancing and singing. Robo holds a speech, how serving humans, can better the relationship of us all, and how children grow up with robots.

Robots also like to meditate, so there is robotic yoga and a meditation course which we can attend, shall we?

Find a comfortable seat, rest your ro-buttocks on the ground and sense the earth. Relax your shoulders and neck, your wrists and whole body, deeply inhale and chant: AUUUMMMMMM.

Robot yoga, meditation and of course the robots celebrate the sunsets, after all the sun light is the benefactor of all. All the robots wave and raise their arms in cheerfulness. Happiness spreads around when all the robots gather to see the last rays of the sun. This spectacle happens everyday, but together, it is just way more fun.

As the sun sets, all join in,
Let the beautiful night begin,
The great sky colored in blue,
Starts to transform, it's true.
Splendid colors, like rose and gold,
Under the eyes of many unfold,
All in awe, stand, wait and bless,
the night is in full progress.

The sun reflects in the hearts of all,
There is just one last call,
To see this wonderful event,
And maybe to make a new friend,
It doesn't matter if human, robot or fairy,
We are all in a way unique and special.

Every single sun beam is unique,
Like every breath of a being,
Hence we are all seeing, likewise and the same,
everyone is different in this one game,
We call it life and it comes with light.
A start to a good, good night.

The first light candles of joy,
Twinkling stars come to the forefront,

As we breathe the last beams of the sun dissolve,
The heaven colors in nice shapes and forms,
The stars laugh from the endless space.
Every individual has a unique face.
We are all one and yet different, isn't that true?
Let's help one another to make dreams come true.

The Robot party is just a start and Robo is one of a kind, thanks to him we could understand how robots work so much, serve and still can party at their Robot Day, isn't that great.

Robots seem to be very happy, that we are there, likewise that nature is there. The sun and the moon, come and go, but we are here to enjoy every moment.

Breathe and feel the body being light and calm. Breathe and sense you are alive, and ready for a good night. Let's leave the Robo family and come to ease, a good night sleep, for peace, love and harmony, dream well and enjoy every moment.

Say goodbye to Robo and help yourself to a nice, soothing rest, oh and maybe this time, leave all your robots out of your reach, this can help for a better sleep. Good night and rest well.

Fairy Stories

1604 words - 23 minutes

In the fairy world we start with the wonders of the forest. This time we come to a wonderful and ancient forest. A forest, we call a city forest, in the midst of an urban jungle, where fairies are rare, but there, there is one of a kind.
 A strong and likewise tender, splendor fairy named Lisa, she gives all to protection and uphold to the forest, to keep the mysteries of the magic dust.

Lisa, the fairy herself grew up in a small village forest close to the city, she knew, one day she has to go to the urban jungle and study or live. However, one night this destiny became a secret opportunity to become a fairy herself.

As her mother always reads mystical and magic stories, LIsa was so intrigued, that she went into the forest by herself to experience what she believed was true. The unique journey of Lisa led her to an entry, a mystical entry where fairies swirled around and there, she asked kindly for permission to have access to the fairy wonder forest.

After decades of living and studying with the forest beings, she discovered, she was not alone. There were young lads who wanted to be elves, and people who practiced yoga within the magic forest. She met dwarfs and unicorns, as well as Giants and Royal Bees, who keep the forest alive and protected.

As she studied she also saw the dark side of the forest, as people chopped trees and harmfully invaded this place of peace, love and unity.

Therefore she knows until this moment, to keep the forest protected is to keep humans in balance. So, she took up the challenge and met with her teachers in a calm Moment to discuss what to do.

These teachers were fairies, and mystical beings that advised her to go back to her hometown to live a secure life, to study and protect the nearby forest for the sake of balance and harmony.

Lisa was very encouraged and helped herself to meet again with all the forest inhabitants to celebrate her last evening in the mystical magical forest.

All her friends in the forest say goodbye and gift her a new magical dust bag, so that you never forget, that living in the forest also means to do service and to collect the magic dust, so you can spread this into the dreams of all children.

Lisa loves children and always likes to enhance the dreams of little ones. Fairies know all the dreams, but they also like to live simple and in harmony with nature. Therefore all her friends stand with her around a fire place and sing her favorite songs:

Oh, LIsa was a fairy,
So kind and oh so dear,
She left the magic forest,
Without the slightest fear.

We can celebrate her here,
Right now, she is free,
And she might be safe,
Wherever she helps.

We fairies like to make dreams come true,
Even better for the world and for you,
We love to keep the secrets of the forest safe,
And follow what our teachers say:

Always be kind, compassionate and brave,
even in the slight struggle, there is a phase,
Up and down, down and up, life goes its way.
Let's live it to our best and pray.

All beings may be safe and sound,
All beings may find a peaceful ground,
All may be protected and secure,
In happiness, peace and harmony.

In circles the fairies dance and sing their songs and the night shall be long, but Lisa knows, when the sun rises, she is off to the forest of her home.

Coming home is something special, it has a specific taste to it and Lisa does like it. The air is fresh where she comes from and the leaves are green.
Breathe in.
Breathe out.

As Lisa enters the forest, she needs a little help, therefore she speaks a prayer:

Oh, may all the beings be with me, may the heaven and earth help me, and hopefully the forest, too!
New experience always need our openness and kindness, but Lisa simply starts to make a fire, like she knows it always to do.
There comes a wolf and greets her kindly.

I am Wolfy and here to protect you, I know you grew up in this region and came back to protect this forest. I am all on your side. Thanks to you, all the forest beings are happy again. Let's make the moment a good one, let's wander through the forest to find a spot for you.

Oh, you like this spot, of course, this is why you are making fire here. Yes, can I serve you some food, or introduce you to the other forest members?

Forests are often very close-nitted communities where there is constant communication. The trees and animals are often very friendly as one is friendly to the animals and trees.

Lisa, I know you are a good fairy, but we have people come here to leave their bad wishes, and this is slowly disturbing the balance of the forest, what can we do?

Lisa thinks wisely and holds space. Bring them here and let me talk to them. There come a wilderer, a wood chopper and a small boy. Let these people be free, and give them a seat. Now, we have to find a peace plan, for you all.
Just meditate with me and you shall never hurt the forest anymore.
We only hurt, when we don't know to feel.
So, let's all sit in peace here for a moment. Wilderer, wood chopper and young boy, please close your eyes and repeat after me.

I am part of this earth-
I am part of this earth.

I am part of this forest,
I am part of this forest.

I ask for forgiveness and mercy-
I ask for forgiveness and mercy.

I shall be thankful for life-
I shall be thankful for life.

And happy that I breathe-
And happy that I breathe.

Thank you kindly, all living beings, let's now meditate in silence and I shall offer my magic ferry dust unto you.

Just breathe gently and slow, kindness is streaming and compassion flows with every single breath. We inhale and sense the forest air, we exhale and feel the love and light.
Inhale love, exhale light.
Inhale Love, exhale light.
Inhale, Exhale, Natural, all natural. In and out.

All is well, the forest is forgiving you, and you can receive the blessings of the forest, just open your hands and close your eyes. Feel the breathing and sense the ground.
Magic dust spreads around the forest, where the fairy Lisa does her first wonder.

These people never ever disturbed the peace of the forest, except for the little boy, who was so curious, he came to her again and inquired, how to be of good statue, helping others to be in balance.

At this moment Lisa accepted Him, Christopher, as a student disciple and they both live in this urban forest to maintain peace and equanimity.

Whenever there is a problem, Lisa is there. She is very kind and evenly helps the forest animals to recover.
One day, Christopher came with a rabbit, which was intensely hurt, but she knew how to heal the rabbit.
Just let him dry in the straw and prepare a soothing tea for the rabbit. A remedy made of leaves and roots will strengthen him.

After one week, the rabbit was healed just with the power of compassion and nature. Lisa works many more wonders and at the same time teaches Christopher all she knows. There came a night, where she was able to give so much magic dust to the people of the city, all the people slept the best sleep ever and healed from many diseases.

Like right now, Christopher and Lisa Are protecting the forest and whenever people come to the forest she teaches how to heal and sleep well. As Lisa knows the importance of the night, she teaches all the visitors how to sleep well.

Lisa explains: Sleep is like making good food. Preparation is everything and one shall know what the recipe says. Is there a recipe, we can follow this every time and the food will taste good every time, hm?
Yes, a good recipe works wonders, so is good sleep depending on a good recipe says Lisa.

One might take a good warm bath, a nice herbal tea infusion, a nice message, good music and a nice good night story. These are perfect ingredients you can mix and choose. Of course a warm hug and guiding presence of a loved one are appreciated as well as the sound of nature. One might sleep best, in nature, with a simple prayer before going to bed.

I Meditate upon the light that is within all the beings,
So shiny and beautiful I bow down to all being,
With gratitude and serenity, I pray for all beings.

Repeat this a couple of times and you shall be ready to go to bed, but even though, sometimes thoughts and dreams come, then, we have to activate our breathing and come back to our natural sense of living. Breathing in and out, it is like heat we are cooking with, we need it to maintain the process.

In the end, we can imagine, there is white, magic fairy dust spread all around our head, eyes, heart and feet. This helps, because magic fairy dust is magic.

Lisa, thank you so much for your advise, Smile and be happy,
Any advice is for free and all is to be happy.
Have a good night, meditate and dream on.

General Boys and Girls Stories.

1504 words - 17 minutes

Two siblings they were so simple and easy going, one was a carpenter and another one was a gold smith. Both liked the adventure and knew, one day, they would discover the world.

Both were very inventive and especially for the big discovery they created a nice suitcase, which was light and comfortable, and could be handled as a bed. Both of the siblings was unique, but they were twins, which makes them both appear likewise.
One was Fred and the other one was Hansen.

Both of the twins loved to be in nature, therefore they packed everything in that suitcase and started to travel the world.

First they begin their journey around the vast ocean where a ferry boat stops and the captain asks: Can I help you, you look like you are ready for an adventure!
Both the twins agree and smile. They enter the ferry and the captain is delighted, I am happy, you are so young and free, I remember when I was your age, I could only go to sea, and this is what I did my whole life. I love the sea and all that comes with it. One time, even, I saw a mermaid and heard her singing the most beautiful songs, it went something like this:

Under the sea,
I keep eternity,
Waters safe,
Endless harmony

The captain smiles and takes the twins unto an adventure over the sea. Telling more stories, the two twins now have a suitcase full of stories.

As the journey goes on, the two twins leave the sea and come to a forest, there an old, wise man sits, with a long white beard.
Have you heard of meditation? I meditate all the time and can show you how to live a healthy life.

The both agree under a tree and listen to the wise meditator.
Just breathe in, and out, meditate upon your heart and feel that you are all a part of this wonderful world, in peace, love and harmony.
Sitting there, one of the twins totally smiles, while the other is extremely calm. The wise forest man is happy, too.

Come on in, I can bring you to the wisest and most precious trees, and of course we can share some stories.
The twins join and share the last stories of the sea man, the ferry ride and the song of the mermaid.

The Forest man laughs so loud that he wakes up the owl and the wolf. Both have been curious, but they just sit and watch. There is the wise man bringing two lookalikes into the forest, to introduce them to the trees. Great!

The Trees are so calm and peaceful. They watch the three meditators with kindness.

We have seen many decades, and many people pass by, but you All are something special, there must be wonderful adventures waiting for you in the mountains. Go and tell the mountain man, that we thank them dearly, for their protection and peacefulness.

The two twins agree and are happy, to bring a message of peace and serenity, from the forest to the mountains, where adventures are waiting for the two.

The forest is leaving them with kindness
Now the great hills await the two,
Always happy to be alive, traveling from sea to land,
And back from land to the mountains.
Always trusting on companionship and friendliness.
Two brothers, Fred and Hansen, great in curiousity.

The Mountain air is fresh and there is a house on the peak of the mountain. Fred breathes, Hansen freezes, keep warm and breathe with me, says Fred, ok, I trust you.
Hand in Hand both hold on to the travel of a life.

When the night comes, they unpack the travel gear with a comfty bed, where both are warm and fed. Always with them, they carry it up the hills, to a small mountain hut, with a lady and 6 girls.

There they are welcome, from the father of the hut. Simple living, simple travel story. The twins leave the message for the peace and good of the woods, the mountain people are happy to receive.

On a warm oven, the stories go on, and the twin tell why they have left home.

We are crafters, to craft a life, but at home, there is always a strive. Who is the better, the one with the art, but we are both one of the same part.

As Twins we know, competition is lost, as soon as you try to win.
Better find a reason, to travel, learn and grow, and life, life will show.
 Why you are here, why you go there, maybe to learn how to blissfully be.

The mountain man looks in amazement and says, you are so brave, please, take the hand of one of my girls. They always look for something new to do, and have never had the chance for themselves to proof.

The twins renounce and smile with joy, let's rather embrace the moment of Now. Breathe and sing, dance and craft, a life is worth so much. The both look at the stars and know, closer to heaven they are for sure.

The 6 girls dance around the living room and the warmth of the space cheers all up, they celebrate life in this small mountain hut.
Until the two ask what to do, maybe we can give you a hand?

The mountain man says, please, spread the message of the peace between mountain, forest and sea, into the wide world, so everyone can see. The whole earth is one, like every single one, we just like to be happy, and in harmony.

The two twins agree and make themselves free, into the world, into the life, to meet and not to strive. With a message of good.

On the hills they look into the horizon, and into one another's eye. Fred and Hansen, smile, what a life, full of surprise.
There shoots a star in the endless horizon, up in the sky, and Fred and Hansen, know this shall be a good, good night.

Fred and Hansen continue on a journey far away, and wherever they stay, they spread the message of good. Everywhere, one rather should, love and unite, in peace and harmony.

From the land, to the sea, from the sea to the land, to the forest, and up the hills. Seeing shooting stars, and a wonderful dance, now Fred and Hansen are making new friends.

In a city so vast, people look at them fast, they know, travelers are always a good show. So, they speak to them, what do you do? Fred and Hansen are kind and tell them what's true.

We have been to far away lands, and everywhere we go, people are kind, and let us know, how beautiful life is.

As we travel, we bring a message of peace, from the forest, and sea, and the mountain hills. Everywhere, there are people, and people are kind. One of a kind, can you see?

Let us all live in Peace and Harmony,
Let us unite in joy and serenity,
May all people come together for a party.

So people like to hear and celebrate with Fred and Hansen, the event of life. All sing and dance in the city streets, with smiles and laughter, upkeeping the Peace. The message is clear, just be harmless and fine, and everything might be align.

Fred and Hansen come to sing in the city streets, along the rivers and streams, back to the source. There waits their father and with much delight. He gives thanks and praises that his Sons are alright.

He hugs them warmly and greets them with a bow, with respect and peace in his voice:

My sons, I have waited for you, such a long time, now that you are back, there must stories to tell, but wait, lets first CELEBRATE.
With a deep breath of relief the father invites the whole party, to come and listen to the story of the world, from the home, to the sea, to the land, the forest, up the hills and what you have heard.

Up the stream, back to the source, all know, Peace is like the travelers way.
The traveler is a guest wherever one may stay.
As the guest follows along, he might be a king,
To the feet of the house, with peace to the door,
Travelers are always one to adore.

Now, that there is time, they give forth their suitcase, with all you need, for a good good sleep.

We receive the case and open it up, a story book and a blanket we got. Always keep it dear and the stories you remind, whenever there is a meeting, you have something to say.
May this travel good night, suitcase, accompany you on your way.
May it be a precious Help and Guidance for each and every Day.

Sleep well and Dream on.
Life has just begun.

www.ingramcontent.com/pod-product-compliance
Lightning Source LLC
Chambersburg PA
CBHW081417080526
44589CB00016B/2568